CASINO HEALTHCARE

The Health of a Nation: America's Biggest Gamble

DAN MUNRO

Dedicated to Kim

Without whose love and support, this book would never have been hatched –
let alone completed.

TABLE OF CONTENTS

PREFACE

Shortly after the release of his book "Flash Boys," author Michael Lewis appeared on *60 Minutes* with Steve Kroft. Early in the interview, Michael described the complexity of high-speed trading on Wall Street in a way that revealed how the activity really worked:

> *"If it wasn't complicated, it wouldn't be allowed to happen. The complexity disguises what is happening. If it's so complicated that you can't understand it, then you can't question it."*[1]

High-speed trading on Wall Street relies on milliseconds to game the whole system, but Michael's quote actually applies more broadly to a wide range of activity in the American economy. In fact, it's tailor made for lots of different segments, many of which are consumer facing—including healthcare.

Whether it's a cable bill or an airline seat, a hotel room or a new car, a home mortgage or a college education, a mattress or a major appliance, American commercial ingenuity has complicated lots of consumer buying and selling activity far beyond the trading desks on Wall Street. The need to do this is obvious even if the methods are totally opaque. Commercial, for-profit interests around consumer choice intentionally complicate the buying process in order to maximize revenue extraction and profits.

Much of this activity is perfectly legal and openly rewarded in a capitalist society and I fully endorse a wide range of consumer price points and choices, but should that include healthcare? In fact, nowhere is the complexity of buying a service more layered, or expensive, than in healthcare,

---

[1] CBS News: 60 Minutes transcript of Michael Lewis interview (original airdate - 03/2014)

which now represents a large and growing portion of most American household budgets. For millions of Americans, health insurance is now the largest monthly expense.

> *"This year my family joined millions of others whose health-insurance premium has become their biggest annual expense. More than our mortgage. More than our property taxes. More than our state income tax. More than our annual food or energy costs."*[2]

As a country, our National Healthcare Expenditure (NHE) will eclipse $3.4 trillion this year—which is effectively more than $10,000 per person. As an industry, U.S. Healthcare is now an economic unit roughly the size of Germany.

An obscure analysis in 2012 by a journalist at The Sacramento Bee revealed an alarming statistic. Million-dollar medical bills in Northern California were on the rise—dramatically. Whether that's scientifically true or not is immaterial. In order to reach a million-dollar hospital bill, you have to gamify every aspect of healthcare, which is exactly what we've done. Like that cable bill or airline seat, we've complicated all of it in a way that defies understanding and then, more importantly, questioning.

This is the story of how the layered complexity of U.S. Healthcare evolved and remains largely intact to this day. In many ways, it's analogous to a big industrial scale casino and to extend the analogy, every major casino has a floor map. This is the floor map for the uniquely American game of Casino Healthcare.

---

[2] Wall Street Journal: $lammed by Obamacare (03/2016)

I.

A CASINO CULTURE

It's a simple, yet pivotal opening question because it's at the very heart of healthcare: *Is healthcare a basic human right or is it a privilege that somehow needs to be earned, or bestowed, and by whom?* How much of our health is the lottery of life itself and how much of it is the lottery of a healthcare system that's been designed to maximize revenue and profits over safety and quality?

This dual-sided nature of luck in healthcare is at first private and deeply personal, but beyond that, it's also systemic and societal. For industrialized and civilized societies, healthcare is a foundational bookend. While education starts at the beginning of life, healthcare is largely the opposing bookend toward the end of life. The questions cascade quickly. How much of each should logically be an individual versus a shared, societal responsibility?

It's all so much of a gamble and while gambling isn't unique to American culture, there's no doubt that it's in our very DNA and we've industrialized it to an enormous scale. This industrialization isn't just in all the obvious places like Las Vegas, Atlantic City or the local Indian casino. Legalized gambling is an engine that drives multiple industries and major cities, even entire states, all across the U.S.

- U.S. Venture Capital (also known as "risk capital") invested almost $60 billion in the startup ecosystem in 2015. About 75% of startups never return their original venture capital.

---

[3] Kasama Project: The reality of US healthcare: Gambling with human lives (05/2015)

- U.S. Casino Revenue is expected to eclipse $22 billion this year.

- Americans are expected to wager over $4 billion on a single game: Super Bowl 50.

- Online fantasy sports "entertainment" will eclipse $3 billion in betting this year.

- State-run lottery revenue was over $70 billion in 2014 (over $200 per capita per year).

This last one is interesting because state-run lottery revenue is now bigger than ticket sales for Major League Baseball, the NFL, movies, music, and gaming software revenue—combined. The housing bubble (as showcased by another Michael Lewis book—The Big Short) was largely fueled by the allure of "quick-flips" for fast profits using "other people's money."

Beyond overt gambling, we've applied the principles of "gaming" to many other consumer experiences as well. From airline seats to cable and cellular bills, pricing is intentionally variable and opaque as the primary mechanism to maximize revenue extraction. Think that passenger next to you on your flight paid the exact same amount for their seat? Guess again.

> *"The price of airline tickets purchased within the same cabin can vary by as much as $1,400 on a single flight, according to a new study. Researchers at Hopper.com this morning said they've confirmed what disgruntled travelers have long suspected: Airlines can charge passengers wildly different rates for seats on the same flight."*[4]

Think there's a single price through a few websites for a hotel room around the world? The new online search site Trivago aggregates pricing information from about 300 other travel booking sites. Prices won't vary as much as the airline seat perhaps, but does a single hotel room really need 300 different booking websites? Of course not, unless there's an alternative need. The

---

[4] ABC News: Airline Ticket Prices Shown To Vary Wildly (08/2014)

need that trumps the simple and transparent is the complex and opaque. It's the game of revenue extraction.

Through the years, we've been sold to think of "gaming" as a business solution to major problems—both at the state level (as a more palatable way for states to raise funds) and then more recently at the individual level as well. Sometimes, we're even encouraged by the herd to gamble. How many of us didn't buy at least one Powerball ticket recently when the jackpot hit a record $1.5 billion?

As consumers, we openly grumble at these obvious tactics which are layered, complex and confusing, but we've come to understand—if not expect them. Consumer advocacy through publications like ConsumerReports work well to cut through some of the complexity with relatively unbiased reviews, but they are unique and it was just this year that they opened up their hospital rating system (by state) for free to the general public.[5]

The question for U.S. healthcare, however, is even more fundamental. Is this model of gaming complexity—largely an artifact and accident of history—truly what's best for the health of a nation? Can a highly complex service—which requires clinical training, demands safety and is heavily regulated—be reduced to a "gamified" consumer shopping experience? Should it be? Can and should we use a commercially-driven model of gaming as the primary mechanism for funding the enormous cost and profits of healthcare? Is this in our collective best interests for the health of an entire nation?

As a consumable product, healthcare is obviously unique in many ways, but at the most basic level, there are actually multiple casinos in play. The first and largest, of course, is the one delivered genetically at birth—the lottery of life itself—but the second is the lottery associated with the healthcare system as available (or denied) to each of us as citizens.

In fact, the system known generally as U.S. Healthcare isn't a single casino at all, but a combination of three distinctly separate ones. The first is the

---

[5] Consumer Reports: U.S. Hospital Rating by State

insurance casino where coverage is sorted largely based on ability to pay. The second is the delivery casino where specialized care is actually received and the third is the pharmaceutical casino—where pricing for life-saving drugs is so variable (based on ability to pay) it might as well be a slot machine. In the pharmaceutical casino, even though health insurance is likely to include a drug "benefit," that's not always the cheapest way to buy the prescription drugs you may need to stay alive.

Surprisingly, it's this highly mechanized and industrial lottery of U.S. Healthcare that often eclipses genetic composition or even personal behavior.

"When it comes to health, your zip code matters more than your genetic code."[6]

Relative to that system, and as evidenced by these sobering statistics, we've reached a saturation point for our "system" that's truly unsustainable.

- National Healthcare Spending (NHE) will exceed $3.4 trillion this year (2016).[7]

- That translates to well over $10,000 per capita per year—just on healthcare.

- NHE is roughly 18% of our entire GDP.

- As an economic unit, U.S. Healthcare is about the size of Germany.

- NHE is currently forecasted to grow about 4% to 5% annually through 2024.

All of which might be easy to comprehend and defend if the results were truly spectacular. Here too, the evidence is sobering.

- Preventable medical errors in U.S. hospitals are now the 3rd leading cause of death in the U.S. (behind cancer and heart disease).

---

[6] Forbes: Top 10 Healthcare Quotes for 2013 (12/2013)

[7] Forbes - U.S. Healthcare Spending On Track To Hit $10,000 Per Person This Year

- Medical debt is a major contributing factor if not the leading cause of personal bankruptcies.

- Across multiple high-profile studies, the amount of money wasted in healthcare is roughly 30-50%.

- Hospital pricing is largely determined by a private syndicate—or cabal—in secret, and beyond legal challenge.

- The pharmaceutical industry—with the highest net profit margin of almost any industry—paid out $15 billion in fines over the last six years, just for off-label drug marketing.

- Driven by pharmaceutical claims of "free speech" under the First Amendment, the FDA has effectively given up on regulating the "off-label" marketing of drugs.[8]

- American healthcare was recently ranked dead last when compared to 10 other industrialized countries.

This gaming mentality extends even further to one of the more onerous references in healthcare: *"Skin in the game."* Beyond just revenue extraction, there's a new expectation that healthcare "consumers" need to be financially rewarded (or punished) for behavior that's often a direct attribute of a socio-economic status, zip code or genetic inheritance.

Through the decades, Casino Healthcare has evolved to be so complex and complicated that many are content to throw up their arms in exasperation and simply claim "it's broken." While this may be a popular consumer or patient view, it's not one shared by industry insiders. A single slide with an insightful quote was delivered by a nationally recognized surgeon (now retired) at a national healthcare conference in Washington D.C.[9]

"The system was never broken, it was built this way"

---

[8] Medpage: FDA Concedes Defeat on Off-Label Drug Marketing (3/2016)

[9] Mary Bourland, MD - National Business Coalition on Health Annual Conference - 2014

Steven Brill captured some of the elements around egregious and exorbitant healthcare bills in his Time cover story *"Bitter Pill,"*[10] but the patient stories he recounts are a single slice at the end of a very long sequence of administrative and financial steps. They are not the whole story for anyone—let alone the whole country. They are like accidents on a freeway. Human nature causes us all to pause and stare, but there's a much larger story that needs to be included. The need for clarity is paramount because our very lives depend on the game mechanics of Casino Healthcare.

Reading Brill we are simply left to conclude that the whole system is like an accident—and clearly broken—when it fact it isn't broken at all. The larger story here is that the system is absolutely opaque and intentionally complex. It's the masterful evolution of maximizing revenue and profits at the expense of safety and quality. This isn't a conspiracy of creation, however, as much as one of prevention and neglect around the kind of reform that can and will build a sustainable healthcare system for an entire nation and for generations to come.

The tendency is to think that because the legislation is so dense and cumbersome that we have a regulatory compliance problem that stifles innovation. The reality is that we have a system of regulatory capture by entrenched incumbents who continue to build large, expensive cost centers (i.e.: hospitals) in search of new revenue streams.

The lottery of life dictates that at some point in every life, we will need healthcare services. These are likely to include expensive treatments, procedures and medicines. Healthcare must work for all of us because at some point in our lives, we (or a loved one) are likely to be totally dependent on the healthcare system to remain alive.

Healthcare reform is already underway, but it will be hard work to successfully challenge the enormous profit centers with equally enormous legal and financial defenses. The Affordable Care Act (ACA or Obamacare) is a great first step out of Casino Healthcare, but it's a single step. More reform

---

[10] Time: Bitter Pill - Why Medical Bills Are Killing Us (04/2013)

will be necessary and that will require more legislation. The size and scope of the challenge is evident in this single quote.

> *"How many businesses do you know that want to cut their revenue in half? That's why the healthcare industry won't reform the healthcare industry."*[11] **Rick Scott**, *Governor of Florida*

Using gaming theory and gaming mechanics, the U.S. healthcare system has really evolved into a giant casino and the stakes couldn't be higher. It's not just our individual health either; it's the health of the entire nation. The systemic design of Casino Healthcare has a number of key attributes.

- An enormous imbalance of doctors—loaded with debt—that are further handicapped by the loss of 10 years of earning power. Of course there's going to be a shortage of the lowest paid specialty—primary care—only a fool would expect otherwise.

- A system of "selective health coverage," unique to America, that uses artificially created filters like age (twice), employment, military service and income for determining subsidized group coverage—and then often spinning this roulette wheel of "enrollment" annually.

- Cabals—like the AMA—that are unofficially allowed to recommend core pricing in ways that have a corruptible influence on the whole system—and remain entirely beyond legal challenge.

- Allowing an accident and artifact of history—employer sponsored health insurance—to remain intact and unchallenged.

- A hospital pricing mechanism called the "chargemaster," which guarantees that the least able to afford expensive healthcare services—those without health insurance—are billed an artificially high amount as a way to maximize the offset to taxable income for a hospital or practice.

---

[11] Forbes - Top Ten Healthcare Quotes For 2012

- Shifting costs in ways that are so opaque, they can't even be reviewed intelligently—let alone questioned.

- Allowing large hospital systems and provider networks to grow in ways that create regional healthcare monopolies.

- A fee-for-service system that still rewards volume over value—and will for the foreseeable future.

- Enterprise billing software that's so expensive, proprietary and architected to process fee-for-service transaction that it's almost guaranteed to maximize revenue and profits

- A system where safety and quality are intentionally difficult and expensive to measure.

With all the exotic allure of a James Bond movie, casinos can be fun. You can win a fortune—or wind up bankrupt—and while they may strip you of your finances and dignity, they are rarely lethal. Casino Healthcare on the other hand, isn't remotely exotic or fun and yet the stakes couldn't be higher. The culture of gambling that's become so pervasive in other elements of U.S. life is quite literally killing us in healthcare.

"Sometimes first class means you get a six-foot-long bed and a large entertainment screen in your personal suite. Sometimes first class means a skinny seat with a slight recline, no entertainment other than jokes from a chatty flight attendant and a snoring seatmate to climb over to get to the bathroom. And sometimes those two extremes are offered on the same route by the same airline for the same price."[12]

II.

THE BIG SORT

As evidenced by the quote above, American industry often relies on complex and opaque pricing games. Whether it's airline seating, cell phone plans, or cable bills, there has to be a tiered pricing model in order to maximize the revenue extraction, and nowhere is this more sophisticated—and complicated—than healthcare.

Our first experience and logical entry point into Casino Healthcare is the casino known as health insurance. In this casino, health insurance is sold by over 900 companies to millions of Americans using a tiered pricing model that's entirely based on ability to pay. In some cases, it's Government-issued (or subsidized) coverage, but it's still health insurance and insurance itself is nothing more than pooled risk. An easier way to think of this tiered pricing model, as applied to healthcare, is what I call "the big sort."

Healthcare, in every part of the world, is expensive, so the only way to avoid the enormous and personal financial risk associated with unforseen and unintended personal healthcare expenditures is with a system of pooled risk, or health insurance. In general, there are only three types of health coverage that a country can implement for an entire population. The two biggest are universal health coverage (UHC) and selective health coverage

[12] WSJ: What Is First Class These Days? It's Complicated (09/2015)

(SHC). The third type is really the absence of either UHC or SHC, and it's no formal system at all. Many emerging or third world countries are stuck with this last one strictly by their limited economic capacity. Healthcare in these countries is typically threadbare and Government-provided or donated, and largely free to the general population through State-run hospitals and clinics.

While it's not formally recognized as a term, I use SHC as a way to compare it to the only other alternative—UHC. That, in turn, is critically important because the U.S remains the only industrialized country with SHC. In fact, every other industrialized country has adopted UHC.

Definitions are critical, but one important aspect of UHC that's often intentionally misunderstood is the fact that UHC is not always "single-payer" healthcare. By definition, single-payer healthcare is UHC, but UHC is often multi-payer and that's a critical distinction for the last chapter—The Road Ahead.

The U.S. may not be a good candidate for single-payer healthcare for many reasons, some of which are cultural, but that doesn't mean it can't implement UHC. Germany and Holland (with impressive metrics across many health categories) are both examples of UHC in a multi-payer system. The U.S. model, however, winds up as the most fragmented and complex of all because it combines both SHC *and* commercial, for-profit insurance companies. In effect, we've designed the most complicated way to adminster healthcare economically because it's the best way to maximize revenue and profits.

First, a definition. This is always easier said than done in healthcare because it's all so politically charged. In fact, each word of UHC is subject to broad and wide interpretation. Still, it's important to start somewhere, and perhaps the broadest definition is the one provided by the World Health Organization (WHO). From their website, WHO frames their definition with the question, "What is Universal Coverage?" The answer, while a tad lengthy, is definitely usable for our purposes here:

Universal coverage (UC), or universal health coverage (UHC), is defined as ensuring that all people can use the promotive, preventive, curative, rehabilitative and palliative health services they need, of sufficient quality to be effective, while also ensuring that the use of these services does not expose the user to financial hardship. This definition of UC embodies three related objectives:

- *equity in access to health services - those who need the services should get them, not only those who can pay for them;*

- *that the quality of health services is good enough to improve the health of those receiving services; and*

- *financial-risk protection - ensuring that the cost of using care does not put people at risk of financial hardship.*

Universal coverage brings the hope of better health and protection from poverty for hundreds of millions of people - especially those in the most vulnerable situations.

Universal coverage is firmly based on the WHO constitution of 1948 declaring health a fundamental human right and on the Health for All agenda set by the AlmaAta declaration in 1978. Achieving the health Millennium Development Goals and the next wave of targets looking beyond 2015 will depend largely on how countries succeed in moving towards universal coverage.[13]

That's a reasonably good definition because it effectively separates coverage from payment. For many countries, payment is often "single-payer," but it can also be "multi-payer," as well. This separation—coverage from payment—is critical to understanding some of the systemic flaws in the U.S. system and just how these flaws are unique to America. It also helps in understanding the complexity of the U.S. system, which remains economically committed to both selective and commerical, for-profit health insurance coverage.

---

[13] World Health Organization: What is universal coverage?

Here's a list of those countries that have formally embraced the principle of "universal health coverage" and approximately when they adopted UHC:

Australia – 1975	Italy – 1978
Austria – 1967	Japan – 1938
Bahrain – 1957	Kuwait – 1950
Belgium – 1945	Luxembourg – 1973
Brunei – 1958	Netherlands – 1966
Canada – 1966	New Zealand – 1938
China – 2009 *	Norway – 1912
Cyprus – 1980	Portugal – 1979
Denmark – 1973	Russia – 1996 *
Finland – 1972	Singapore – 1993
France – 1974	Slovenia – 1972
Germany – 1941	South Korea – 1988
Greece – 1983	Spain – 1986
Hong Kong – 1993	Sweden – 1955
Iceland – 1990	Switzerland – 1994
Ireland – 1977	UAE – 1971
Israel – 1995	U.K. – 1948

Of course there's a big asterisk and tons of ambiguity for China and Russia because statistics for both countries are shrouded in politics and controversy. Actual numbers are difficult to locate and verify. A November 2012 report by McKinsey, for example, offered the following summary for China:

> *"According to official government statistics, public health insurance covered 95 percent of the population by the end of 2011; the actual figure is probably lower because some people with multiple types of public health insurance would have been counted more than once."*[14]

---

[14] McKinsey & Company: Health care in China: Entering 'uncharted waters' (Nov, 2012)

In describing healthcare in Russia, Wikipedia suggested the following opening sentence:

> *"The Constitution of the Russian Federation provides all citizens the right to free healthcare under Mandatory Medical Insurance in 1996."*[15]

For Russia, the financial burden of this "free healthcare" was clearly evident when Vladimir Putin announced a 2% increase (from 3.1% to 5.1%) in the obligatory medical insurance tax paid by companies (2010).

In the cases of both Russia and China, the challenge is arguably the quality of healthcare that is delivered under the terms of "universal coverage."

So, if America is reliant on SHC and multi-payer, how is this different than UHC (either single or multi-payer)? It really starts with the whole selection process that we have for buying (or receiving) our health insurance coverage. We sort people into different categories of health insurance coverage— or none at all (a category we call the "uninsured"). There's a lot of churn between the categories for several reasons (time, income, employment etc. …) so the numbers are hard to pin down with real precision and they are in constant flux, but here's a list of the general categories by coverage type and approximate number.

Selective Health Coverage by Type	
Medicaid/CHIP	60,000,000
Medicare Only	49,800,000
Dual Eligible	12,000,000
Individual ACA Exchange	10,400,000
Individual Non-ACA Exchange	8,100,000
Indian/Alaskan/State High-Risk	2,000,000
Total Public Enrollment:	**142,000,000**
Employer Sponsored Insurance	113,100,000

---

[15] Wikipedia: Healthcare in Russia

Military (VA & DoD)	14,100,000
Fed/State/Municipal	21,800,000
Total ESI Enrollment:	**149,000,000**
Total Public Enrollment:	142,000,000
Total ESI:	149,000,000
Uninsured Children (under 18)	5,000,000
Uninsured Adults (over 18)	25,000,000
Total U.S. Population (07/2015):	**321,000,000**

The actual numbers are both a compilation and an estimate—with a lot of help from a source with impeccable credentials for this—Charles Gaba. He's become an industry insider for the most reliable numbers around Obamacare signups and that's also the name of the website where he posts all the most up–to–date charts. We collaborated for the chart above—based loosely on research that he did for a comparative analysis between 2013 and 2015.[16] He described his difficulty with this aspect of his research in a separate email.

> *"There's really no single, best source for this data and it has already stirred some controversy within the policy community. If it's this hard to agree on numbers within insurance categories, I can only imagine how difficult it is to administer all the different groups—both at the front-end of healthcare and then again on the back-end. It's not just qualifying or paying to participate in one of the categories, it's the whole billing process that all the providers have to go through after healthcare is actually delivered. It's just mind numbing in its complexity and I don't think we'll ever get to a consensus on the numbers. In part because there's a lot of churn among the categories—some of which occurs throughout the year and some of which occurs organically within both the annual open*

---

[16] ACASignups.net: Total U.S. Coverage Status 2013 - 2015

enrollment and public categories. In terms of both provider networks and consumer coverage the churn is constant and significant."[17]

In the end, the individual numbers for each category aren't as critical as the sheer number of categories. As if to actually embrace and emphasize complexity, we sort by multiple categories.

- Age (twice—either over 65 or under 26)
- Military service (VA)
- Low Income (Medicaid)
- Employment (Employer sponsored insurance—or ESI)
- Public Service (municipal, county, state and federal employees)
- Time (annual enrollment)
- Temporary coverage (COBRA—guaranteed coverage for 18 months between employers)
- Location (often by state—based on access to provider network associated with a benefit plan)
- Emergency medical condition (EMTALA)
- Charity care (for the uninsured—or often simply underinsured)

Of course the administrative burden to all this sorting is just enormous—in every direction—and the bulk of it starts with an annual (and uniquely American) process called "open enrollment." The open enrollment process for health insurance coverage under Obamacare in 2016 began November 1, 2015 and ended on January 31, 2016. Open enrollment for employer-sponsored-insurance (ESI) is often limited to just a few weeks and often occurs in the fall for the following calendar year of coverage.

It's during this "window" that Americans must select their "plan." The plan itself has critical variables that affect not only the cost, but also which providers (and hospital systems) are considered "in-network." It's this in-network designation that's critical in terms of which providers and services

---

[17] ACASignups.net: Author Charles Gaba

will be considered covered and paid for by the insurance company under terms of the policy.

The other variables that affect the cost of health insurance directly are the number of covered lives (single or household), the amount of the annual "deductible," and the type of coverage (narrow or broad network).

The provider "networks" are also highly variable based on opaque negotiations between insurance companies and the doctors that agree to pricing based on commercial insurance rates. There are no negotiating rates for Medicare or Medicaid, but commercial rates are whatever the market between doctors and commercial insurance companies will support—by city and state—down to individual zip codes.

All of which creates a casino-like atmosphere based on variables like plan level, type, networks, deductibles, and co-pays. How this game is played by consumers will determine the monthly premium costs for the calendar year ahead. Agents, brokers and "guides" are available to help with the decision tree around affordability, but the ultimate variable—how much life-sustaining or life-saving healthcare anyone needs in a given year—is the largest single component and it's a big unknown. A single heart attack, stroke or cancer diagnosis could easily eclipse the healthcare needs in every other year of life—combined.

The complexity doesn't end here, of course, because the billing for healthcare services is totally dependent on the type and nature of insurance coverage—so all of the front-end sorting complexity is then duplicated on the back-end—healthcare delivery. The cost to administer this labyrinth of payers and networks on the part of providers isn't trivial.

> "$84,000. Of all the eye-popping numbers I came across while researching why the United States has the most expensive health care system in the world—and why my company, MCS Industries, Inc. has faced double-digit health insurance rate increases year after year—that's the one that shocked me the most. **Every physician in this country now has to**

spend $84,000 a year, on average, just to interact with private health insurance companies.[18]

This isn't just physicians and clinics, its hospitals too. In fact, hospitals have entire departments that do nothing but interact with all the commercial insurance companies and consumers over billing and payment issues.

By comparison, countries that have "universal health coverage" have almost none of this "network" or dual-sided cost complexity. Even countries with multi-payer systems don't have anywhere near this enormous complexity for an entire country with millions of highly mobile people—across 9 times zones and 50 states—including the ritual and annual churn called "open enrollment."

The last two sort categories of coverage—EMTALA and Charity care—require a little more detail.

Several times over the course of his 2012 Presidential bid, Mitt Romney suggested that emergency care in America is a form of universal healthcare coverage. I first heard the reference during a 60 Minutes interview he did with Scott Pelley.

> **Pelley:** *"Does the government have a responsibility to provide health care to the 50 million Americans who don't have it today?"*
>
> **Romney:** *"Well, we do provide care for people who don't have insurance, people—we—if someone has a heart attack, they don't sit in their apartment and die. We pick them up in an ambulance, and take them to the hospital, and give them care. And different states have different ways of providing for that care."*[19]

Less than a month later, at a meeting with the Editorial Board of the Columbus Dispatch, Romney doubled-down on his 60 Minutes remark.

---

[18] Fix It - Healthcare At The Tipping Point: Richard Master letter

[19] CBS 60 Minutes: Campaign 2012 (09/2012)

"We don't have a setting across this country where if you don't have insurance, we just say to you, 'Tough luck, you're going to die when you have your heart attack.,' No, you go to the hospital, you get treated, you get care, and it's paid for, either by charity, the government or by the hospital. We don't have people that become ill, who die in their apartment because they don't have insurance."[20]

Donald Trump has mirrored this view with his proclamation that under his administration, "there won't be people dying in the streets." It's important to understand what both of these candidates are referencing here because many Americans believe they represent a kind of "universal health coverage" when, in fact, they don't.

What Romney and Trump are referencing is a law known as the Emergency Medical Treatment and Active Labor Act (EMTALA[21]) which was passed in 1986. This unfunded mandate stipulates that hospitals are legally required to provide care to anyone needing emergency treatment regardless of citizenship, legal status or ability to pay. But here's the kicker—*there are no reimbursement provisions for healthcare provided this way. Hospitals don't receive payment for much of the healthcare that they deliver through their emergency departments.*

The cascading consequences of EMTALA are often unspoken or ignored outright, but they are significant.

- Since there is nowhere to send these bills, hospitals use a bookkeeping entry called "uncompensated care." According to the American Hospital Association (AHA), uncompensated care through the years has mushroomed to over $80 billion per year— just through hospitals. The amount through other channels is largely unknown.

---

[20] The Columbus Dispatch: Romney in Central Ohio | Health care called 'choice' (10/2012)

[21] Health Law Resources - Emergency Medical and Labor Treatment Act (EMTALA)

- Over the course of 35 years, the combined amount of uncompensated care delivered through American hospitals amounts to over $700 billion.

- This isn't entirely negative to the hospitals because they leverage this category of expense as an offset to profitable income for tax reporting purposes.

- For 2013 alone, uncompensated care was estimated at $85 billion.[22]

The effect is that we're all paying for this particular game of 3-card Monty— not once, but twice. Once through the higher premiums for our own insurance coverage, and then again through higher taxes as an offset to the reduced taxes paid by hospitals.

Hospitals don't simply provide ANY care through their emergency department, but they are legally required to provide *"an appropriate medical screening examination within the capability of the hospital's emergency department, including ancillary services routinely available to the emergency department, to determine whether or not an emergency medical condition (EMC) exists."*[23]

If the hospital staff determines that it's not an EMC, which is well within their legal right, then the patient is discharged, even if the health condition is unresolved.

A great example of just how this ER door can become revolving is the lowly toothache. As anyone who's ever had a serious one can attest, these can be quite severe and will easily prompt someone to seek medical care through a local emergency department. But this is not considered an EMC and hospitals have no dentists. The primary cause of the pain is often an abscess and the emergency department treats these with a pain medication and antibiotics (which is largely inappropriate and ineffectual). Patients are then discharged with the unhelpful instruction to "see a dentist." Of course if they

---

[22] Health Affairs: An Estimated $84.9 Billion In Uncompensated Care Was Provided in 2013 (05/2014)

[23] Health Law Resources: EMTALA

could afford to see a dentist, they would have done that to begin with and probably long before the tooth was so painful that they wound up seeking relief through an ER.

> *"There are nearly 1 million Americans who visit the emergency room each year because of dental pain at a cost that runs into the hundreds of millions."*[24] **Miles O'Brien – Frontline Correspondent**

For lack of dental insurance coverage, dental pain isn't treated by a dentist who is trained to actually solve the condition, but through the emergency department where the only remedy is temporary relief of pain. The actual abscess remains and almost guarantees a return visit to the ER.

The effect of EMTALA as an unfunded mandate has been so severe on some hospitals that they've been forced to simply close their emergency department altogether. The rate of these closures has been on the rise. According to a JAMA study released in 2011, the number of Emergency Departments (EDs) in metro areas from 1990 to 2009 declined 27%—representing a net loss of 667 ED's.[25]

Some ED closures may well have been necessary, but for millions of uninsured (and underinsured) Americans, EMTALA and the ED is often their only healthcare option—except for one final category of healthcare delivery—charity care.

The last big sort on the delivery side of Casino Healthcare is—and always has been—a sizable commitment by a variety of charitable organizations to provide totally free or charity care. For those who can get access to this, it's a very real lifeline, and it's truly free healthcare (to the extent that the cost can be covered by the charity). One of the more recognized in this category is St. Jude's Children Hospital and there are dozens—if not hundreds—of others. One of these is an organization founded by Stan Brock that provides totally free, charity care.

---

[24] PBS Frontline: Dollars And Dentists (06/2012)

[25] JAMA: Factors Associated With Closures of Emergency Departments in the U.S. (05/2011)

Stan's about eighty years old now, so he should be fully retired, but he's not. In fact, he has no money to speak of, no bank account and often sleeps on a rolled up mat he carts around in his travels. His face is weathered and etched today, but if the name's familiar, it's because he once personified the role of dashing adventurer in the popular television series known as Mutual of Omaha's Wild Kingdom. If there was ever a direct source of Spielberg's Indiana Jones character—Stan Brock might well have been it.

About thirty years ago, Stan founded an organization called Remote Area Medical (RAM). As a very real bush pilot, he thought it would be great to combine his piloting skills with those of health professionals who could be dropped into disaster sites and remote parts of the world with free healthcare. His original thinking was that this would be helpful for places in sub-Saharan Africa—or Haiti—or maybe the Amazon jungle. Places he was very familiar and comfortable with as he traveled the globe for Wild Kingdom. In some ways, it was just a natural extension of both his youth and his life on the TV series.

He was right of course, but what he found was startling because the need for RAM wasn't actually as great in other, impoverished parts of the world as it was right here in the U.S.

RAM has now served over 500,000 Americans with free healthcare. Most of the healthcare that RAM delivers is dental or vision, but they offer other services, too. RAM does this with week-end clinics around the country. While many Americans are lining up for Apple's latest gadget, tens of thousands line up for a very different, but necessary luxury: free healthcare.

There's clearly a rich and colorful history to our system of selective health coverage, but it's not remotely a function of design as much as evolution. No one sat down and said *"as a country, this is what we need and want."* The system isn't broken; it's just struggling under the enormous weight of patches and legislative band-aids like Medicare, Medicaid, CHIP, EMTALA, and COBRA that evolved over the decades.

The President's signature legislation—The Affordable Care Act (or Obamacare)—is really just another in this long line of legislative band-aids.

It has made some improvements around the edges of healthcare, but not at the core. The changes brought about by Obamacare aren't designed to address and will not solve some of the larger systemic flaws.

> *"We don't need to put 30 million new people in the same [insurance] maze. We need to first figure out [our healthcare system] and improve it."* **Mark Bertolini** – *Chairman and CEO of Aetna*[26]

The evidence of failure for our system of selective health coverage is multi-directional, except one. It continues to generate enormous profits for a long list of insurance companies, providers, REITs, pharmaceutical companies, attorneys, med schools, medical device manufacturers, and the large hospital systems across the country.

In terms of design, there probably isn't a more complex way to administer healthcare for any size country, let alone one with 320 million people. This administrative complexity isn't just at one end of the system. It applies to both the front–end (coverage) and the back–end (delivery) of healthcare.

There's really no one to blame. It's simply the product of evolution, not intelligent design. The hope has always been that free-market principles would magically correct any inefficiences and could be applied or molded to healthcare in the same way that they apply to other sectors of our "free-market" economy. The hope was that competition would create downward pressures on pricing like they do for other services and commodities.

That left the door open for a system to be optimized for revenue and profits, not safety and quality. The fact is, the system is performing as designed and that includes the first and largest variable into the whole system—The Big Sort. Like a casino with different "games" for different "players," our healthcare system has sorted coverage into tiered delivery entirely on the ability to pay. The trouble is, the companies holding all the cards in Casino Healthcare aren't remotely interested—or incentivized—to change the first "house rule." That rule is how coverage and delivery are sorted.

---

[26] Medical Economics: HIMSS Keynote: Aetna's Bertolini calls for transformative healthcare change (02/2014)

"There is no method to the madness. As we went through the years, we had these cockamamie formulas. We multiplied our costs to set our charges." **William McGowan,** *CFO UC Davis Health System (and 30-year veteran of hospital financing)*[27]

III.

THE BIG SHIFT

While it's tempting to discount the above quote due to age (2004), it's important to understand that nothing inside hospital pricing has really changed. The Affordable Care Act included some pricing experiments—and CMS has announced a shift toward "value-based" payments—but the core pricing mechanism for America's 5,700 hospitals remains largely intact. At the very foundation are billing codes for services and supplies combined with a few new ideas on how to group or bundle fee-for-service pricing.

Electronic health record software was largely designed to accommodate this primary healthcare function—billing—and EHR software (as it's come to be known) continues to do that today. These software installations for accounting and health record management are so large and unwieldy that it will literally take an act of congress to change it.

The previous chapter covered the American system of "selective healthcare coverage," or what I call The Big Sort. While every other industrialized country has standardized on "universal health coverage," America still sorts coverage by fairly arbitrary categories like age, income, employment, military service, geography and time. This front-end complexity also extends to the back-end of healthcare (delivery) with a corresponding and equal force.

Once we actually need real healthcare (not the low-acuity retail pharmacy type), there's an immediate need for billing to reconcile the various

---

[27] WSJ - California Hospitals Open Books, Showing Huge Price Differences (12/2004)

categories of selective coverage to a specific price in a way that's ultimately profitable for the doctor, provider or healthcare facility. In order to keep the doors open at the hospital, the various types of coverage all have to be matched to pricing and then combined in a way that generates a profit. The only way to do this at scale is through a mechanism I call "The Big Shift."

Some have disputed the degree by which this variable pricing happens— and there are market nuances like geography and population that play a large role as well—but no one disputes that variable pricing is alive and well in the largest single category of U.S. healthcare spending—inpatient hospital care.

While there are many distinct categories of healthcare spending, by far the largest is inside America's 5,700 hospitals. Hospital spending accounts for about 32% (almost 1/3) of our entire National Healthcare Expenditure (or NHE).

By the time we add the outpatient costs that are connected to inpatient care (including prescription drugs); it's easy to see how hospital care is probably closer to 50% or more of all healthcare spending. If we're trying to make a dent in the cost of care, hospital spending is by far the largest component. But hospital pricing is totally opaque.

The first piece of this puzzle is to understand just how widely variable U.S. hospital pricing is compared to other countries. Here are a few examples, but there are literally thousands of others.[28]

---

[28] The New York Times: The $2.7 Trillion Medical Bill (06/2013)

Angiogram	Colonoscopy	Hip Replacement	Lipitor (Rx)	MRI Scan
Avg. U.S. Price	Avg. U.S. Price	Avg. U.S. Price	Avg. U.S. Price	Avg. U.S. Price
$914	$1,185	$40,364	$124	$1,121
Canada	Switzerland	Spain	New Zealand	Netherlands
$35	$655	$7,731	$6	$319

The evidence of exorbitant pricing is in every direction and from every source—even if it's not new or newsworthy. Looking at the raw data, many will argue that pricing transparency will bring much needed competition to an isolated (and opaque) market and that exorbitant pricing will quickly collapse. The key assumption to that narrative, of course, is that hospitals are lucrative and have sufficient capacity to flex pricing quickly in order to avoid a perception of "medical gluttony" (as originally outlined by Dr. Otis Brawley in his book "How We Do Harm"[29]).

Certainly some hospitals, and by extension hospital systems, are wildly profitable, but many are not. According to Delos Cosgrove (CEO and President of Cleveland Clinic) almost a quarter of American hospitals are losing money.

> *"Healthcare is a low-margin economic activity. Enterprises of this kind are vulnerable to even minor fluctuations in the economy, much less the seismic shifts we're seeing in healthcare finances today. Almost a quarter of American hospitals are already losing money. With that number bound to increase in coming years, we already know what to expect because we've seen it before in the airline, supermarket, phone and*

---

[29] Amazon: How We Do Harm by Otis Brawley, MD

electronics businesses. There will be a wave of mergers and acquisitions to improve quality and lower costs."[30]

This dire assessment is easily confirmed by data from both the American Hospital Association and healthcare consultancy Avalere Health. While the number of community hospitals with a negative operating margin is higher, the number with a negative total margin is about 25%.[31]

This narrative is important for the argument that a relatively small, but global consulting firm called L.E.K. makes relative to shifting costs inside hospitals.

> *"The unique American hybrid payer system (with limited direct out-of-pocket payments) creates complexity, mixed incentives and uneven quality and outcomes. Major change is underway, but the history of healthcare teaches us that evolution trumps revolution. We know the U.S. system will migrate away from fee-for-service toward outcomes and quality, but this will be an uneven ride by geography, provider type, and overall impact on members."*[32]

As a global consultancy across many industries, L.E.K. publishes many research reports for the various sectors—including healthcare. One such report from 2013 was intriguing in both its assessment and forecast. The balance of this chapter is loosely based on this report—Hospital Economics and Healthcare Reform[33] (May of 2013).

The summary is worth quoting verbatim (bold emphasis added).

> *"Conventional wisdom holds that U.S. hospitals will be net beneficiaries of healthcare reform. After all, hospitals currently care for many patients who are uninsured and cannot pay their medical bills. As the*

---

[30] LinkedIn: The Great Consolidation Begins by Toby Cosgrove (03/2013)

[31] American Hospital Association: Percentage of Hospitals with Negative Total & Operating Margin (02/2015)

[32] L.E.K. Consulting website

[33] L.E.K. Consulting: Hospital Economics and Healthcare Reform (PDF report)

Affordable Care Act (ACA) moves more people into insurance coverage, hospitals will be reimbursed through Medicaid for these patients."

"However, this conventional wisdom is contingent upon a key assumption: that the uplift from Medicaid expansion will overcome other negative macro forces that will simultaneously affect hospitals in the same time period. In this new Executive Insights, L.E.K. Consulting examines the impact of healthcare reform and other approaching macro forces in sequence. ***According to our analysis, the net impact of legislative, structural and demographic factors in the wake of healthcare reform will be materially negative for most hospitals in the country."***

"The authors argue that hospitals will face such acute pain in the future that they and every other player in the healthcare value chain will be forced to innovate and create new paradigms in order to survive. The authors conclude by identifying the strategies that leading hospitals have developed to prepare for their challenging future."[34]

The case that L.E.K. makes is compelling because it highlights what many already know to be true about hospital pricing, namely, while exorbitant pricing is certainly provocative (especially as more of it becomes visible), it is actually well founded on hardcore economic realities. Those realities are based on the economic necessity of shifting costs based on coverage type (as determined by "the big sort"). They are relegated to this accounting slight-of-hand just to maintain the "low-margin economic activity" referenced by Dr. Cosgrove.

This concept of "cost shifting" is best seen visually in this chart.

---

[34] L.E.K. Consulting: Hospital Economics and Healthcare Reform (report webpage)

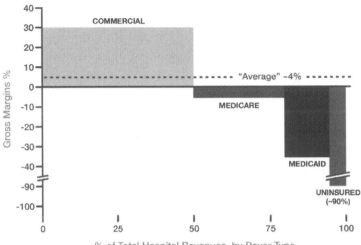

% of Total Hospital Revenues, by Payer Type

There is no other single chart that helps to explain with simple clarity the pricing challenge inside every hospital. Forgetting for a moment that this chart represents Gross Margin exclusively (independent of taxes or tax consequence), every hospital has four general and distinctly different "buckets" of revenue:

1. The uninsured (**negative** margin)
2. Medicaid (**negative** margin)
3. Medicare (**negative** margin)
4. Commercially insured (positive margin)

In effect, hospitals only have one category of positive margin, or profit and it's exclusively derived from those patients who are commercially insured. The rate charged to this one profitable group is entirely dependent, therefore, on how much negative margin is accrued by the other three categories—and that is entirely dependent on other variables like geography and patient demographics. When you average the margin across all four categories for this fictitious suburban community hospital, it equals a somewhat paltry 4%. It's relatively easy to see from this one chart the direct correlation to and variability with commercial premium rates (independent of the negotiating power of any one payer or employer).

L.E.K. is not alone in this assessment. In fact, L.E.K's data is in very close proximity to that compiled separately by the American Hospital Association and the healthcare consulting firm Avalere Health.[35]

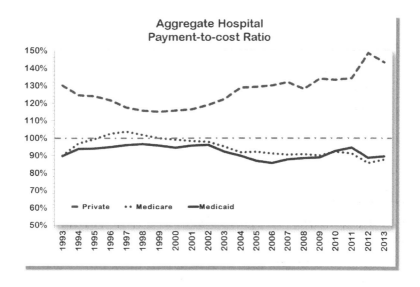

In this chart, the lines represent payment-to-cost ratios for the three biggest buckets: Private Payers, Medicare, and Medicaid (unlike L.E.K., they simply omitted the uninsured as a 4th category). With cost represented at 100%, Private Payers deliver about 40% profit, but Medicaid and Medicare are both negative, at about 10%. The volume of Medicaid, Medicare (and uninsured) negative margin is what dictates pricing (and requisite profits) through Private Payers, but it's largely designed to simply keep the doors open (or return a modest 4% average profit).

---

[35] American Hospital Association: Aggregate Hospital Payment-to-cost Ratios (PDF)

Once again we see how private, commercial payers compensate for the other sources of revenue. Other than a relatively brief period (from about 1995 through 2000), margin dollars from Medicaid and Medicare have both been negative.

The Lewin Group performed a similar analysis for the Arizona Chamber of Commerce in 2007 (published in 2009).[36] To the extent that the amount of negative margin (in the categories of Medicare, Medicaid and the Uninsured) increases, there's a corresponding "hydraulic" increase that's necessary in commercial (private) insurance rates.

Variable pricing on delivery of healthcare isn't, in fact, some great mystery; it's tied directly to selective health coverage—The Big Sort. The extent by which the costs are "shifted" isn't uniform, but it too has an anchor. That anchor is the combination of geography and demographics surrounding the delivery facility itself. Things like age, economic tier and employment play heavily into the coverage variables—which directly impact the price.

Many argue that "cost-shifting" isn't universally true which is correct. Many hospitals don't "cost-shift" or don't "cost-shift" enough—which is why so many (about 25% according to Delos Cosgrove) are operating in the red and why hospital consolidation is accelerating. Cost-shifting is not a uniform behavior, but it is absolutely widespread—especially among the large, profitable hospital chains like HCA, CHS and Tenet.

> *"We found that fifty US hospitals had charges that, on average, were ten times their Medicare-allowable cost. These hospitals' charge-to-cost ratios were more than three standard deviations above the US average, which suggests that they are outliers and warrant additional scrutiny. Our analysis showed that forty-nine of these fifty hospitals are for-profit, forty-six are owned by for-profit hospitals systems, twenty-five are in just one for-profit system, and twenty are in Florida."[37]*

---

[36] The Lewin Group: Analysis of Hospital Cost Shift in Arizona (03/2009 - PDF)

[37] Health Affairs: Extreme Markup: The Fifty US Hospitals With The Highest Charge-To-Cost Ratios (06/2015)

Pricing aside, the administrative burden of this price shifting on the back-end (delivery) of healthcare is staggering. Hospital billing—by far the largest single component of all healthcare costs—revolves around what coverage to apply and which network has been negotiated by which carrier. The problems that cascade from this are evident in multiple ways:

1. Systemwide inefficiency, waste and abuse (as measured across six studies) ranges from 27% to 53%.

2. Billing fraud—estimated at between $98 and $272 billion each year.[38]

3. Electronic health record software that's been architected to optimize the complexity of all this billing (that churns annually) for episodic, fee-for-service care (where more episodes of care—needed or not—equate directly to more revenue and profits).

4. Pricing information that—when available—has no real cost-accounting.

5. All of which combined represents the largest single component—about 1/3—of our entire national healthcare expenditure every year.

As costs have escalated, the stampede for pricing transparency in healthcare has taken on the aura of a full crusade and it does sound both logical and appealing. It enjoys widespread and enthusiastic public support. In fact, a kind of cottage-industry has blossomed around providing Americans with visibility into the opaque pricing madness, but pricing transparency does absolutely nothing to change the underlying economics of how variable pricing is created—and needed in our system of selective health coverage.

The demand for pricing transparency makes us feel good, but that feeling is falsely based on the assumption that pricing is egregiously high everywhere—and that simple visibility will foster competition and swift pricing correction. It won't.

---

[38] The Economist: The $272 Billion Swindle (05/2014)

This isn't to say that we shouldn't make systemic changes to low-acuity, primary care—we absolutely should, and many of these are either here or in the pipeline. Retail clinics, telehealth with online consults using primary care physicians or nurse practitioners, and smartphone-based clinical support are making important contributions and will have an impact, but the ROI timeline is long. Even in combination, any economic gain of these efforts is easily eclipsed by the annual growth of healthcare spending (about 4-5% through 2024).

All of which suggests that whatever we may think of exorbitant hospital pricing, at least according to one global consultancy, the forecast ahead won't include dramatically lower prices. What seems to be more likely is what Delos Cosgrove suggested in his article from March of 2013—an era of consolidation.

> *"Bigger isn't always better, but when it comes to healthcare we're finding that it usually is. Doctors, hospitals and medical centers across America are looking for ways to collaborate, consolidate and merge their resources. They're discovering that high volume medical centers can produce better outcomes for many procedures, and more effectively and efficiently provide care across a whole spectrum of services. Medicine is becoming a team sport."* **Delos Cosgrove** – *CEO and President at Cleveland Clinic*[39]

This brings us full circle to a second quote in that Wall Street Journal article from 2004. Again, it's dated, but so little has changed since then that it still applies to The Big Shift.

> *"The elaborate pricing systems hospitals have developed over the years will be difficult to change. The entire system will have to be blown up."* **Jan Emerson** – *spokeswoman for the California Healthcare Association*[40]

---

[39] LinkedIn: The Great Consolidation - Toby Cosgrove, CEO and President at Cleveland Clinic

[40] WSJ - California Hospitals Open Books, Showing Huge Price Differences (12/2004)

"For the past decade, all wage increases have been absorbed by rising healthcare costs."

Don Berwick – Former CMS Administrator[41]

IV.

THE BIG SQUEEZE

Many of the headlines in healthcare are particularly sobering—including this one from the Washington Post in the fall of 2015.

Health plan deductibles are growing seven times as fast as wages[42]

The chart used in the article captured the drama with visual simplicity.

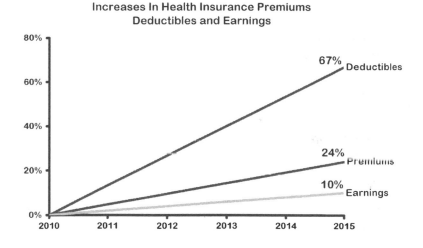

Increases In Health Insurance Premiums
Deductibles and Earnings

---

[41] SAS Health Care & Life Sciences Executive Conference: Keynote May, 2012 (pdf - slide #3)

[42] The Washington Post: Health plan deductibles are growing seven times as fast as wages (09/2015)

More generally, the cost for healthcare for all of us has been rising dramatically for well over a decade.

The actuarial firm of Milliman Incorporated publishes an annual index known simply as the Milliman Medical Index. The firm itself isn't well known outside of healthcare circles, but it was established in 1947, so it's just one year shy of its 70th Anniversary. Here's a brief background from their website:

> *From its inception, the firm was a leader in life insurance and pension consulting, and later grew robust healthcare and property & casualty disciplines. In the 1950s, Milliman issued the first health insurance cost benchmarking tool, which continues to be the most respected pricing tool available. In the 1960s, Milliman consultants pioneered new designs for annuities and employee benefit plans and helped devise the first health maintenance organizations (HMOs). In the 1970s, Tom Bleakney and Wendell Milliman literally wrote the book on public pensions. In the 1980s, Milliman developed early pension valuation and financial modeling systems that would become industry standards. In the 1990s, the firm began its global expansion by opening an office in Tokyo, and that expansion has now culminated with Milliman offices in most major cities around the globe. And in the last decade the firm has eclipsed $750 million in revenue while continuing to be an innovation engine for our clients.*[43]

The point is that the firm has compelling credibility and subject matter expertise for a very specific index, one they call the Milliman Medical Index (MMI). It's even more dramatic than the one by Kaiser/HRET for deductibles because it's the average cost of healthcare for a fictional American family of four with employer-sponsored PPO insurance coverage. Here's the chart for the MMI through 2015.[44]

---

[43] Milliman website (history)

[44] Forbes: Annual Healthcare Cost For Family Of Four Now At $24,671 (5/2015)

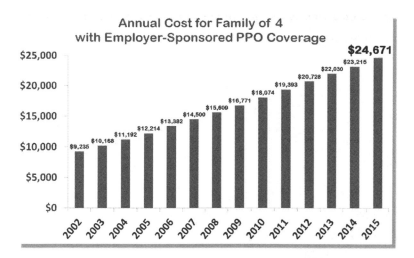

In fairness, this is the combined amount of all healthcare costs for both the employer and the employee, but the employee portion—both payroll deductions for insurance premiums and out-of-pocket expenses—have been on a very similar upward trajectory. In 2015, just the employee portion of healthcare costs for our fictional American family of four surpassed $10,000 annually for the first time and the six-year trend suggests that 2016 will easily eclipse $11,000 per year.

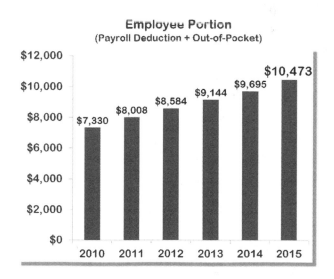

That translates to roughly $873 per month for our fictional family of four. For many American families, this is almost guaranteed to be the second highest monthly expense behind mortgage or rent.

When politicians or economists talk about "bending the cost curve" in healthcare, the Milliman Medical Index is rarely referenced and yet it's among the most important charts of all when it comes to average Americans who are left to foot the enormous—and growing—healthcare bill.

In fact, headlines through much of 2014 and 2015 were eager to celebrate the fact that the growth of healthcare costs had been effectively stopped and there is truth to that claim. The forecast for 2016 through 2024 is a relatively narrow range of 4-5%.[45] In 2002—one of the highest on record—the annual growth of health spending was a whopping 8.6%.

While this lower growth rate is certainly good news, it's not remotely helpful to consumers and patients who are left to foot the enormous bill. A 4-5% growth rate is encouraging to politicians and economists who then breathe a collective sigh of relief relative to the national economy, but the effect on consumer wallets is zero.

The MMI is the most obvious and visible example of this big consumer squeeze because it's direct. The calculation is easy to see and understand, but there are other, more subtle techniques, as well.

The first and most direct way to make monthly premiums more afford-able is to change the amount of the upfront deductible. These plans—called High–Deductible Health Plans (HDHP)—are increasingly popular as a way to lower the monthly expense. It's analogous to the car dealer who steers the buyer away from the total price of the car toward the lower monthly payment. It's a slow—but very real degradation of the insurance product itself and the result is a product that's really only useful in truly catastrophic illness. General health insurance, with broad coverage, is quickly becoming "catastrophic only" coverage.

---

[45] Peterson-Kaiser Health System Tracker (2015)

"In many states, more than half the plans offered for sale through HealthCare.gov, the federal online marketplace, have a deductible of $3,000 or more, a New York Times review has found. Those deductibles are causing concern among Democrats—and some Republican detractors of the health law, who once pushed high-deductible health plans in the belief that consumers would be more cost-conscious if they had more of a financial stake or skin in the game."

"We could not afford the deductible," said Kevin Fanning, 59, who lives in North Texas, near Wichita Falls. "Basically I was paying for insurance I could not afford to use." He dropped his policy.[46]

The very backbone of health insurance—the "indemnity plan" (where coverage was almost total for every doctor and hospital)—was all but completely phased out by 2013.

In 2006, only about 3% of all covered employees were enrolled in HDHP's. According to the world's largest human resources consulting firm— Mercer—in less than ten years, that 3% mushroomed to almost 25%—literally a quarter of all covered employees.[47] This shift continues unabated.

PPO's—which represent the largest single category of plan type (almost 60%), are also under direct assault. Historically, these types of plans were reasonably flexible with coverage outside of the plan's network. That flexibility included paying a portion of the bill and putting a cap on how much a policy holder was required to pay for "out-of-network" care. Those days are coming to swift end.

"Forty-five percent of the silver-level PPO plans coming to the market for the first time in 2016 provide no annual cap for policyholders' out-of-network costs. Not having a cap could lead to tens of thousands of dollars in bills for patients who are hospitalized or treated by providers who are not part of the plan's network."

---

[46] The New York Times: Many Say High Deductibles Make Their Health Law Insurance All But Useless (11/2015)

[47] Mercer: CDHP Enrollment Chart [Figure 3]

> *"Not having any maximum cap on those costs "is what you expect ... in a plan that doesn't offer out-of-network benefits," said RWJF researcher Katherine Hempstead. "You're paying a deductible and then some kind of co-insurance ad infinitum. The average PPO for sale in 2016 is less comprehensive than what was called a PPO in 2015."*[48]

Yet another way that consumers are feeling the pinch is through their employer. Historically, the rise in health care cost has been a shared commitment between the employee and their employer. That effectively ended in 2011. Today, employers are simply pushing more and more of the health-care cost increase directly to their employees.

> *"The actual reason why employee and employer costs are increasing at different rates is because employers have, over time, shifted greater responsibility for health care expenses to their employees through higher deductibles, higher copayments, and higher coinsurance – a practice that began long before the passage of the ACA."*[49]

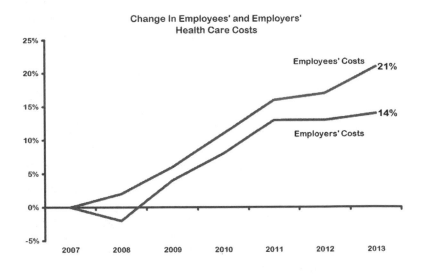

---

[48] Kaiser Health News: 2016 PPO Plans Remove Out-Of-Network Cost Limits (12/2015)

[49] Center for American Progress: The Great Cost Shift - pdf (03/2015)

In effect, employers stopped participating in the rising cost of healthcare benefits and started (around 2011) to simply pass the bulk of the increase directly onto employees.

Another big trend—as a way to shift the ever increasing cost burden—is to create "narrow" networks. Many have compared this approach to the Health Maintenance Organization (HMO) model that was created in the 1970's but quickly fell out of favor by the late 1990's.

The idea behind narrow networks is to limit the number of providers that are available under a given plan as packaged and then sold by the insurance carrier. The health insurance plan that consumers are being sold isn't just pooled risk, it's the added (and totally opaque) risk of the network associated with the plan.

Just as healthcare pricing generally is an opaque and bottomless pit—this form of squeezing has its own form of hidden financial risk in the form of steep "out-of-network" charges.

In her excellent series in The New York Times called "Paying Till It Hurts," Elisabeth Rosenthal highlighted one such case. It's a kind of end-run around the system designed to maximize the billable charges and revenue—typically for expensive surgeries in hospitals.

> *"Before his three-hour neck surgery for herniated disks in December, Peter Drier, 37, signed a pile of consent forms. A bank technology manager who had researched his insurance coverage, Mr. Drier was prepared when the bills started arriving: $56,000 from Lenox Hill Hospital in Manhattan, $4,300 from the anesthesiologist and even $133,000 from his orthopedist, who he knew would accept a fraction of that fee."*

> *"He was blindsided, though, by a bill of about $117,000 from an 'assistant surgeon,' a Queens-based neurosurgeon whom Mr. Drier did not recall meeting."*

"I thought I understood the risks," Mr. Drier, who lives in New York City, said later. *"But this was just so wrong—I had no choice and no negotiating power."*[50]

Where narrow networks have really started to take off are in those plans sold on the public exchanges, as a way to (finally) address the one segment of the market that insurance carriers loathed and avoided for years: the single market.

In this market, it's very difficult to price an affordable premium because the risk to the insurance provider is so different than the pooled or group market. The risk is literally associated to one individual—which could have any number of serious health ailments in a short timeframe—even overnight. The financial gyrations that have evolved in attempts to address this large and growing market are similar to those that were tried in the housing industry—before the collapse. Some of the larger ones include:

- Risk Corridors: where the government agrees to subsidize the cost of premiums by specific location which is known to have higher concentrations of those with medical conditions or need (and therefore result in higher insurance costs to start).

- Narrow networks: whereby providers who deliver actual healthcare participate in selective networks of coverage as offered (and sold) by more than 900 insurance companies.

- Tiered plans: categorized by medal designators like Bronze, Silver, Gold and Platinum—with varying premium and out-of-pocket expenses.

- Non-compliant plans: with significantly lower pricing and coverage (allowable in 21 states through at least 2016).

---

[50] The New York Times: After Surgery, Surprise $117,000 Medical Bill From Doctor He Didn't Know (09/2014)

Often, the information provided to consumers about the "network" associated with the plan they've purchased on either the state or federal exchange is totally inaccurate or woefully out of date.

> *"For the second time in a year, consumer advocates have found that the specialists listed as available to those who bought health insurance on the state exchange aren't all that available."*

> *"When the advocates tried to call the obstetrician-gynecologists in the online directory of insurers' in-network providers, they found the list so outdated that only about 22 percent of the 1,493 practitioners were accepting new patients, performed well-patient visits and had appointments available within four weeks."*

> *"More than a third of OB-GYNs weren't available at all because they had left the networks, retired or were dead — such as Nikita Levy, the former Johns Hopkins gynecologist who killed himself in 2013 after police opened an investigation into allegations he had taken pictures and videos of his patients during pelvic exams."*[51]

Sadly, many are content to assume that a monthly expense of $873—the average cost of healthcare for our fictional family of four—is affordable for most. According to a report released by the Federal Reserve in May of 2015[52], it's an irrationally optimistic assumption.

- Forty-seven percent of respondents say they either could not cover an emergency expense costing $400, or would cover it by selling something or borrowing money.

- Thirty-one percent of respondents report going without some form of medical care in the twelve months before the survey because they could not afford it.

---

[51] The Baltimore Sun: Advocates find problems with lists of health exchange's OB-GYNs (11/2015)

[52] Federal Reserve: Report on the Economic Well-Being of U.S. Households in 2014 (05/2015)

- Just under one-quarter of respondents indicate that they or a family member living with them experienced some form of financial hardship in the year prior to the survey.

The whole point of health insurance is to avoid catastrophic financial events—or bankruptcy—due to expensive (and largely unforeseen) medical expenses.

A study by NerdWallet in 2014[53] estimated that 60% of personal bankruptcies were the result of unpaid medical bills. A summary of the findings included this list:

- Americans pay three times more in third-party collections for medical debt each year than they pay for bank and credit card debt combined.

- 63% of American adults indicate they have received medical bills that cost more than they expected.

- Between 2010 and 2013, American households lost $2,300 in median income, but their healthcare expenses increased by $1,814.

So, what should Americans expect in 2016 and beyond? I posed this question to one of the analysts at Milliman.

> *"The good news is that the annual rate of increase for consumers has been declining for years. The bad news is that healthcare still represents a major component of many American families' household budgets and there are few other household expenses that faithfully increase at the rate of four-figures per year. As evidenced by the index for the last 12 years, American households should continue to expect rising healthcare costs as an ongoing part of their annual budget process."* **Chris Girod** – *Principal and Consulting Actuary at Milliman, Inc.*

In ways that are both clearly visible and totally opaque, Americans are literally being squeezed out of affordable healthcare. In Casino Healthcare, it's the big squeeze.

---

[53] NerdWallet: Medical Debt Crisis Worsening Despite Policy Advances (10/2014)

"Essentially, we sit down with [RUC] every year and say, 'here's $43 billion and grow-ing, how do you want to [divide it]? What's the relative value of weights between anes-thesiologists, gastroenterologists, surgeons?' and set the relative values at what the physician community thinks the relative payment should be." [54]

V.

THE PRICING CABAL

The above quote sure doesn't sound like a very scientific or financially pru-dent way to set pricing for healthcare services and that's because it isn't.

As we learned earlier, of all the trending (and trendy) topics in U.S. health-care, none has more consumer interest and appeal than "pricing trans-parency." Major publications announce its arrival with banner headlines and whole companies have formed to sell us this highly prized informa-tion in a crude effort to sow a kind of consumer revolt. If there's an "Occupy Healthcare" movement, a primary source of its attraction is the totally opaque pricing that healthcare has enjoyed for decades.

The history behind this obfuscation is relatively easy to understand. If healthcare pricing is so large that patients must rely on third-party insur-ance companies for the lion's share of the enormous bill, why bother dis-closing the price to patients at all? Since the price that hospitals and doctors charge is largely dependent on individual types of coverage, there's never been an incentive to disclose pricing to patients. Patients pay a relatively small and fixed deductible (or co-pay). Health insurance companies then

---

[54] American Academy of Family Physicians: What Every Physician Should Know About the RUC (02/2008)

pay the big (and variable) balance. So it has been and always shall be—except that consumers are starting to feel saturated by their annual health-care costs—and they have rightfully started to demand more transparency.

State legislators are considering changes, but the results so far are abysmal. One organization monitoring legislation on pricing transparency just issued their 3rd annual report card.[55] Only five states got a grade other than "F." In fact, one state, Massachusetts, went from an "A" the previous year to an "F."

In early 2013, Steven Brill's cover story for Time introduced us to a price list inside every hospital known as the "chargemaster." By any definition, this "price list" is largely the product of accounting fiction. Some hospitals even publish their price list online. One example of this is Banner Health—a large hospital system with headquarters in Phoenix, AZ. They publish what are called "Direct Pay" prices for a wide range of both inpatient and outpatient procedures by location.[56]

The math for "transparent" pricing works for other purposes, mostly around avoiding taxable income, but it's devoid of any real economic accounting. Even the name—"chargemaster"—is relatively unique to healthcare.

Pricing is so shrouded in mystery and intrigue that a single headline, "Bitter Pill," detailing exorbitant hospital bills based on the chargemaster database captured unprecedented public interest. That cover story by Steven Brill for Time Magazine became the 2nd largest selling story in their history—eclipsed only by the assassination of JFK.

---

[55] Health Care Incentives Improvement Institute – 50 State Report Card on Price Transparency Laws, 2015

[56] Banner Health: Hospital - Inpatient Direct Pay Prices (Arizona)

Up until Brill, the chargemaster was largely an obscure, private database maintained by each hospital as a kind of full "retail" (or "direct pay") price list. Some have compared the chargemaster to MSRP pricing for cars, but that's not a fair comparison. At least MSRP has real economic cost variables behind the publicly available numbers. No such luck with the chargemaster. Across more than 5,700 hospitals throughout the U.S., no two chargemasters are alike.

It gets worse. In a particularly gruesome irony, the patients who are billed at the highest possible rate—the full chargemaster price—are those who can least afford it, the uninsured. These are the patients who are least likely to afford any healthcare price at all, let alone a fictional and maximum "retail price." This perversion—where those least likely to afford any healthcare are charged the highest—only exists in America. It's also why medical expenses remain the leading cause of personal bankruptcy. The hospital logic is simple—since we know we won't be able to capture any revenue from those who are uninsured, let's charge the highest fictitious rate possible so that we can maximize our offset to taxable income.

The goal of making hospital pricing more transparent—including chargemaster pricing—is a noble one even if it's hopelessly naïve. The idea, of course, is that if healthcare pricing were visible and transparent, we could wistfully bring "free market" economics to bear. That, in turn, would somehow defy all logic of supply and demand or cost and value. The result (in theory) would be sweeping and desperately needed pricing relief. As patients, all of us could then easily shop for healthcare services in much the same way that we shop for Lasik, cosmetic or (sometimes) bariatric surgery. Buying a knee or hip replacement could all be done online with Amazon ease and Yelp ratings.

At least that's the theory behind "pricing transparency"—and the hope. It's definitely a big hope.

To begin to remove some of the mystery, I'll start with a simple question. Where does healthcare pricing originate in the U.S.? If you did read Brill's article Bitter Pill, you know that the chargemaster is the exorbitant price list for every hospital and it really only applies to the uninsured, but how is pricing determined for everyone else—including the bulk of the profits—private insurers? Or better yet, how is pricing determined for the largest single buyer of all healthcare in the U.S.—the federal government through Medicare?

We're a market-driven economy and healthcare is largely a "free market," so who exactly is the "market maker?" For a system that will clock in at $3.4 trillion this year, this seems like an incredibly important and fundamental question.

Surprisingly, the principal organization that calculates pricing for almost all of U.S. healthcare is a little-known cabal. Say what? How can that be? First of all, what the heck is a cabal?

> *A **cabal** is a group of people united in some close design together, usually to promote their private views or interests in a church, state, or other community, often by intrigue.*[57]

There's certainly lots of intrigue here, starting with a relatively obscure (and comparatively tiny) organization with a really bulky name: the **AMA / Specialty Society Relative Value Scale Update Committee.** Today it's known less formally as the Relative Value Scale Update Committee—or simply RUC (pronounced "ruck"). There are 31 doctors on this committee and they are associated with all the different specialties that healthcare represent. Specialties like dermatology, neurology, pediatrics, radiology and family physicians each have a representative member.

Now granted, there is no legal definition of a cabal, but here are ten reasons why the RUC certainly appears to qualify as one:

---

[57] Wikipedia - Cabal

1. The RUC is a private organization created (in 1991) by the AMA— itself a private organization.

2. Membership in the RUC is reserved for "Member" Societies and is by "invitation only."

3. Meetings are all held under terms of a rigorous Non-Disclosure Agreement (a "gag order" if you will).

4. The RUC meets three times a year—and meetings are not open to the public or media.

5. The Medicare Physician Fee Schedule (PFS)[58] is based on recommendations made by the RUC—including the Current Procedural Terminology (CPT)[59] codes.

6. As the copyright owner, the AMA also derives a significant portion of its annual ($71M in 2001[60]) revenue from CPT licensing royalties. The CPT codeset represents a monopoly on data used by both the public and private healthcare system in the U.S.

7. Historically, "value" recommendations made by the RUC to CMS/ Medicare for pricing CPT codes have been accepted 87.4% of the time.[61]

8. Private insurance companies (Aetna, Cigna, UnitedHealth, Blue Cross, etc…) use the Medicare Physician Fee Schedule to base much of *their* pricing on these same code sets (PFS & CPT).

9. As evidenced by a lawsuit filed in August 2011[62] and dismissed in 2012, the RUC appears immune to any legal challenge.

---

[58] CMS.gov - Physician Fee Schedule

[59] Wikipedia - Current Procedural Terminology

[60] Public Citizen Health Letter (Nov. 2012) - The AMA and Its Dubious Revenue Streams

[61] HealthAffairs - In Setting Doctors' Medicare Fees, CMS Almost Always Accepts The RUC Advice on Work Values

[62] District of Maryland Court Filing - Center for Primary Care v. CMS and HHS

10. The entirely opaque formula that the RUC uses for all its "value" recommendations is proprietary (meaning they alone use it) and includes a final, mysterious calculation called the "conversion factor."

$$\frac{\text{Work RVU}^1 \text{ x Work (GPCI)}^2 + \text{Practice Expense (PE) RVU x PE GPCI} + \text{Malpractice (PLI) RVU x PLI GPCI}}{}$$

= Total Resource Value Unit (RVU)
X
(2013 Conversion Factor of $34.023

= Medicare Payment

In the most convenient sleight–of–hand, the RUC determines the value for all of the variables in the equation. There is no outside, independent review—and even if there was, the math works fine. The critical question becomes how a group of medical societies, meeting secretly can determine pricing for the largest single payer in the healthcare system—the federal government (Medicare).

All of which makes RUC the de-facto standard of all U.S. Healthcare pricing. It's not just a form of price fixing, it's the very definition of it.

> *DEFINITION of "Price Fixing": Establishing the price of a product or service, rather than allowing it to be determined naturally through free-market forces.*[63]

Relative to that one lawsuit brought against the RUC in 2011, the money quote by the Judge in the dismissal was this one:

---

[63] Investopedia - Price Fixing

"Congress has precluded courts from reviewing, not only the final relative values and RVU's but also the method by which those values and units are generated."[64]

The word "value" is visible and often repeated, but that doesn't mean it's applied to either the pricing calculation or the recommendation to Medicare. At least not in a way that anyone outside of the cabal can understand—including judges. We'll simply never know.

The opportunity for the RUC to run amok with this power and influence is enormous—including one of the few examples that did become public. The article—"The World of Healthcare Pricing"—offered a rare glimpse into a presentation that was made by Dr. Richard Waguespack to the RUC on behalf of his specialty group, the American Academy of Otolaryngology (Ear, Nose and Throat).

According to the article, Dr. Waguespack was presenting a new procedure to the RUC for sinus surgery that involved using an expensive ($2,600) balloon. The RUC arrived at a price ($3,000) for each procedure—which assumed that each procedure used a new balloon. In practice, however, it was common knowledge—and perfectly acceptable—to reuse the balloon up to six times (with proper sterilization we presume).

Six procedures using just one $2,600 balloon could then charge Medicare the full $18,000. Instead of making only $400 profit on each of six procedures (or $2,400 total), the real profit is $15,400, a net difference of $13,000.

That $13,000 profit is effectively endorsed *and* encouraged by the RUC because it's the only billing option for the sinus procedure with that balloon. The author of the article interviewed an actual member of the RUC— Charles Koopmann, MD.

> *Dr. Charles Koopmann has served on the RUC for 20 years, or as long as there's been a RUC. So, he's got a lot of experience with valuing codes. He is also the lone Ear Nose and Throat doctor on the RUC—which means*

---

[64] Senior US District Judge William M. Nickerson Opinion - May, 2012

that if anyone in the room that day [of Dr. Waguespack's presentation] might have realized that doctors could use the same balloon multiple times, it would have been him.

Koopmann: *"Did it enter my mind? It really didn't. All we wanted to do is make sure that the costs got covered for a sinus that you were operating on. And, um, that we were successful in. And it turns out we were awfully successful!"*[65]

There are about 8,000 CPT codes alone and hundreds of thousands of variables (like the sinus balloon) that are used to calculate pricing for procedures.

Roy Poses—an MD and Clinical Associate Professor of Medicine at Brown University—summarized his view this way:

"Economists have beaten us over the head with the idea that incentives matter. The RUC seems to embody a corporatist approach to fixing prices for medical services to create perverse incentives for physicians to do more procedures, and do less conversing with and examining patients, examining the best clinical research evidence about their problems, and rigorously thinking about how best to help them. More procedures at higher prices helps physicians who do procedures. It may help even more the corporations that provide the devices and drugs whose use is necessitated by such procedures, and the hospitals who can charge a lot of money as sites for performance of procedures. If we do not figure out how to make incentives given to physicians more rational and fair, expect health care costs to continue to rise while access and quality continue to suffer."[66]

And that's exactly what healthcare pricing has done—and will continue to do—indefinitely. The government forecast for healthcare spending is projected to be almost $5.5 trillion by 2024.

---

[65] Marketplace: The world of health-care pricing - Gregory Warner (06/2012)

[66] Health Care Renewal - US Senate Subcommittee Asks What the RUC is About (01/2013)

The questions cascade quickly.

If the underlying pricing mechanism is determined in secret and beyond legal challenge, how and when do we fix that—and shouldn't that be a top priority?

- Aside from trying to get more pricing uniformity (which is definitely a good thing), what are we hoping to achieve with this new insistence on "pricing transparency?"

- Assuming every healthcare price was publically available online tomorrow—what then?

- How does pricing transparency end the influence of the RUC?

- More importantly, how will pricing transparency help us in our ultimate quest for healthcare value?

- The list of unanswered questions is long—including this last one.

Do we really need more healthcare pricing transparency, or do we need to get the RUC out of the business of secretly fabricating healthcare prices—by and for doctor's—for the whole system?

Every casino has a "house" that sets the odds. Given the power and influence of the RUC, the AMA by extension is effectively the house in America that sets pricing for much of Casino Healthcare.

"The [Supreme Court] ruling raises the question of why, uniquely in the industrialized world, Americans have for so long favored an arrangement in health insurance that endows their employers with the quasi-parental power to choose the options that employees may be granted in the market for health insurance."[67] **Uwe E. Reinhardt**

VI.

THE ORIGINAL SIN

This book is not intended to be a policy or history book, but there's no way to avoid the history behind one of the biggest, systemic flaws that remains a significant impediment to healthcare reform progress to this day. For lack of a better expression, many simply call it the "original sin."

Like most healthcare systems around the world, ours was never really designed from whole cloth. Through the decades it's evolved primarily through a series of legislative acts that were implemented to fix what often amounted to a single, sizable, and painfully evident problem.

The two most significant legislative acts that Americans are now familiar with are Medicare and more recently Obamacare, and both were designed to address the growing crisis of citizens without health insurance—the uninsured. But the history behind both goes back even further.

The idea of a national health system starts in earnest in the early 1900's, but the idea of health insurance for the elderly—those over 65—first took legislative shape during the Truman administration. It was then argued forcefully by his successor, John F. Kennedy.

---

[67] The New York Times: The Illogic of Employer-Sponsored Health Insurance (07/2014)

"We are behind every country pretty nearly in Europe in this matter of medical care for our citizens."

John F. Kennedy – May, 1962[68]

Among the many motivations for Kennedy's effort at that time was a national survey showing that 56% of Americans over 65 didn't have health insurance. While it would take another four years for final passage of Medicare, the bill's narrow defeat during Kennedy's administration was a significant blow—both politically and personally.

"Of all his narrow losses, the most discouraging to him was the defeat of his "Medicare" bill – the long-sought plan enabling American working men and women to contribute to their own old-age health insurance program under Social Security instead of forcing them, once their jobs and savings were gone, to fall back on public or private charity. The cost of his own father's hospitalization made him all the more aware of how impossible it was for those less wealthy to bear such a burden. The Medicare bill was lost, and he went immediately on television to declare that this 'most serious defeat for every American family' would be a key issue in the fall campaign. The 87th and 88th Congresses would in time pass more health care legislation than any two Congresses in history – including landmarks in mental health and mental retardation, medical schools, drug safety, hospital construction and air & water pollution – but the President never got over the disappointment of this defeat."[69]

There's a much more detailed, and succinct, history of American healthcare (from the late 1800s through Medicare) that was delivered as a talk by Karen S. Palmer at the spring meeting of Physicians for a National Health Program (PNHP) in 1999.

"In 1946, the Republicans took control of Congress and had no interest in enacting national health insurance. They charged that it was part of a large socialist scheme. Truman responded by focusing even more

---

[68] Kennedycare – Fifty years before Obamacare, JFK had his own health care debacle. Slate

[69] Kennedy - by Ted Sorensen (p. 342-344 - January 1, 1965)

*attention on a national health bill in the 1948 election. After Truman's surprise victory in 1948, the AMA thought Armageddon had come. They assessed their members an extra $25 each to resist national health insurance, and in 1945 they spent $1.5 million on lobbying efforts which at the time was the most expensive lobbying effort in American history. They had one pamphlet that said, "**Would socialized medicine lead to socialization of other phases of life? Lenin thought so. He declared socialized medicine is the keystone to the arch of the socialist state.**" The AMA and its supporters were again very successful in linking socialism with national health insurance, and as anti-Communist sentiment rose in the late 1940's and the Korean War began, national health insurance became vanishingly improbable. Truman's plan died in a congressional committee."*[70]

The rise—and ultimate passage—of Medicare is an important aspect of the history of American healthcare because the arguments against Medicare (and more generally, against national health insurance) remain unchanged to this day. The primary argument is always steeped in forceful anti-socialist or anti-communist rhetoric.

All of which makes Medicare an interesting and important chapter in our healthcare history, but it's not the original sin.

The original sin I'm referencing is "employer sponsored insurance," or ESI. While most associate the first employer sponsored health coverage with Kaiser Permanente in the late 1930's, one of the first employers to extend this kind of benefit directly to their employees was actually Montgomery Ward in 1910.[71] While this was the initial spark, it would take another thirty-two years to become the roaring fire that today includes (arguably) over 110 million Americans (roughly one-third of the U.S. population).

---

[70] PNHP: A Brief History: Universal Health Care Efforts in the US (spring 1999)

[71] Bureau of Labor Statistics: The development and growth of employer-provided health insurance (03/1994)

The framing for ESI began just before World War II and it was called catastrophic health insurance. The irony is that just as high-deductible health plans are increasingly popular today (see previous chapter—The Big Squeeze), that's also how health insurance in the U.S. started—as catastrophic-only coverage. We've effectively come full circle.

This evolution began in 1940. At that time, only about 12 million Americans—just over 9% of the total population of 132 million—had some form of health insurance coverage. This made sense in that most healthcare was sufficiently low-cost and could be paid for out-of-pocket.

By 1950, a short 10 years later, about one-half of the population had some form of health insurance coverage.[72]

What caused this explosive growth (from 9% to 50%) in health insurance? A single piece of federal legislation (with an unwieldy name) that's rarely referenced known as **"An Act to Amend the Emergency Price Control Act of 1942, to Aid in Preventing Inflation, and for Other Purposes."** The legislation was passed on October 2, 1942. Literally the next day, then President Franklin D. Roosevelt effectively froze wages with Executive Order 9250 Establishing the Office of Economic Stabilization.[73]

The primary purpose of the act—and the Executive Order—was to freeze wages as a way to quickly and effectively stop inflation. From the Executive Order:

> *TITLE.II*
> *Wage and Salary Stabilization Policy*
>
> *1. No increases in wage rates, granted as a result of voluntary agreement, collective bargaining, conciliation, arbitration, or otherwise, and no decreases in wage rates, shall be authorized unless notice of such increases or decreases shall have been filed with the National War Labor*

---

[72] Monthly Labor Review - March 1994 - The Development and growth of employer-provided health insurance

[73] The American Presidency Project - Franklin D. Roosevelt

Board, and unless the National War Labor Board has approved such increases or decreases.

The whole intent of the Act, of course, was clearly stated in the official name—to stop inflation—but it also left the door wide open for an unintended consequence. That consequence was using benefits instead of wages as a way to compete for a shortage of labor. ESI was officially born and the fact that there were ancillary tax benefits to both employers and employees was simply adding gasoline to the early stages of a small brush fire.

As mentioned in an earlier chapter (The Big Sort), the varying forms of ESI account for almost 150 million Americans. What started as a tax break has morphed into the largest single pool of health coverage for most Americans—health insurance that is provided by their employer.

As with many new markets, at first there was no downside—only an upside.

- Employers had an effective enticement other than wages to attract and keep talent.

- Employees had a real benefit for unforeseen (and rising) health expenses that—at least up until then—were largely paid for out-of-pocket.

- At least in theory, it was a tax benefit to both sides. [No one noticed or paid much attention to the corresponding effect of reduced wages]

- At the outset, monthly deductions for health insurance were relatively small and the "contributions" were conveniently deducted from the paycheck.

- The nascent health insurance industry had a whole new product to sell into an eager and large market.

What could possibly go wrong?

The downside would take about seven decades to become crystal clear—and painfully visible—which is about where we are today. The scope and scale of the exasperation is evident with simple quotes like this from 2012.

When an employer sits down with his health care providers—the broker, the health plan, the physician, the hospital, the drug and device firms—everyone in the room wants it to cost more—and they're all positioned to make that happen.[74]

In general—it's easy and logical for healthcare to evolve as a three-party system; the patient, the provider and the payer (aka the insurance company). Adding an employer to this mix effectively makes it a four-party system which has grown way beyond any usefulness toward keeping inflation at bay during WW II.

The employer tax exclusion alone equates to about $500 billion each year in lost tax revenue. By extension, this tax relief is effectively "the nation's second largest entitlement."[75]

It's also a major contributing factor to rising healthcare costs. As long as ESI is an obscure and opaque "benefit," buried as a line-item deduction on a payroll stub, actual pricing is totally elastic and will scale to whatever "the market" can bear. Using the Milliman Medical Index (from an earlier chapter – The Big Squeeze), that payroll deduction for an average American family of four with employer sponsored PPO coverage is now over $530 per month—just for the insurance premium.

As companies downsized for one of many market conditions, a major flaw appeared—and like Medicare—the flaw was addressed through federal legislation. This flaw was the lack of insurance portability for the employee during gaps or transitions in employment. COBRA was signed into law in 1985 as a way to "continue" coverage for a period of 18 months (in most cases—and up to thirty-six months for widows) until a new employer could provide new (and different) coverage. The patch was sufficient to keep everyone in this game of musical chairs.

---

[74] Forbes: Top Ten Healthcare Quotes For 2012 (12/2012)

[75] Forbes: If Republicans Delay The Cadillac Tax, They Will Cost Taxpayers Far More In The Long Run (12/2015)

The major downsides to COBRA were conveniently ignored in the race to patch the flaw.

1. A relatively short fuse of "extended" coverage (18 months).

2. Loss of the employer-subsidized portion of the premium cost.

3. Abandonment of coverage once the full price of coverage was realized.

With continually rising health care costs, this left a growing number of Americans disenfranchised from coverage altogether—and by extension—access to affordable healthcare. Many who were terminated from employment due to market conditions beyond their control and couldn't afford COBRA coverage were left to join the ranks of the uninsured. By 2013, the number of uninsured Americans swelled to almost 60 million.

The problem today is that we've reached a level of market saturation. The roulette wheel is about to stop and the most important players (the insurance companies, the providers and the employers) are still trying to decide if they want to bet on red or black.

The best example of this saturation is the chart that appeared in an earlier chapter—The Big Squeeze.[76]

---

[76] The Washington Post: Health plan deductibles are growing seven times as fast as wages (9/2015)

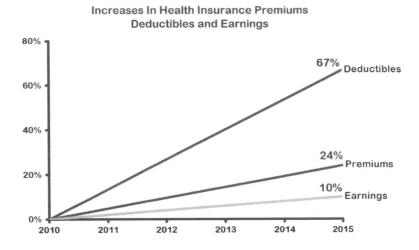

Increases In Health Insurance Premiums
Deductibles and Earnings

While premiums may have been tolerable historically, deductibles (a key component cost of insurance) have exploded. In a sad, twisted irony of history, we're right back to where we started in 1940 when the primary value to health insurance was catastrophic only coverage. Everything else is self-funded.

The problem with catastrophic-only coverage is fundamental to all of healthcare. It's typically cheaper—often by an enormous amount—to catch health problems early in their evolution and most certainly NOT when they've become an emergency or catastrophic health condition.

Former Governor of Oregon John Kitzhaber described a dramatic variation of this conundrum with his "air-conditioner" story.

> *"Here's the air conditioner story: There's a 90-year-old woman with well-managed congestive heart failure who lives in an apartment without air conditioning. That's actually the whole story."*[77]

---

[77] The Washington Post: Is the future of American health care in Oregon? (05/2013)

It's not the whole story, of course, but it's a great lead-in and based loosely on Dr. Kitzhaber's own personal experience as an emergency room physician. The now famous punchline is this:

> *"A hot day could send the temperature in her apartment high enough that it strains her cardiovascular system and kicks her into full-blown congestive heart failure. Under the current system, Medicare will pay for the ambulance and $50,000 to stabilize her. It will not pay for a $200 window air conditioner, which is all she needs to stay in her home and out of the hospital. The difference to the health-care system is $49,800. And we could save that $49,800 without reducing her benefits or her quality of life."*[78]

It's a dramatic example of how it's cheaper—often exponentially—to solve healthcare challenges outside of the healthcare system before they become catastrophic.

This maps directly into the whole world of medical knowledge around major health conditions like cancer, heart disease and stroke—and the enormous cost of treatment.

ESI is an original sin for primarily four reasons:

1. America is the only industrialized country that uses this type of health insurance coverage.

2. Pricing is totally opaque in almost every direction.

3. In an attempt to reign in spiraling healthcare costs, employers are pushed further and further into the business of actually managing healthcare delivery.

4. As difficult as a 3-party system (payer, provider and patient) is to navigate and manage, a 4-party system is simply impossible without major compromises to one (or more) constituents.

---

[78] The Washington Post: Is the future of American health care in Oregon? (05/2013)

President Obama acknowledged the original mistake as a fundamental basis for his signature legislation The Patient Protection and Affordable Care Act—Obamacare:

> *"It's a historical accident that in this country health care is attached to employers. So what we said was we need to set up a mechanism to pool people who currently don't have health insurance so that they have the same purchasing power, the same leverage that a big company does when they're negotiating with the insurance company." President Barack Obama*[79]

That's largely the function of Obamacare—to extend coverage to what had become an enormous number of people (almost 60 million) without afford-able health coverage. The legislation had four large levers to accomplish this.

1. A requirement for everyone to buy health insurance (the individual "mandate").

2. A fine or penalty for those who didn't buy health insurance (through the IRS).

3. A federal subsidy (tiered by income) to make individual health insurance affordable.

4. Expansion (originally to include all states) of Medicaid (health coverage for the poor).

While the net effect of Obamacare is largely positive, it's nowhere near enough, and the ranks of employers who also see the failure of ESI are growing. Employer sponsored insurance isn't just an artifact and accident of history. When it comes to building Casino Healthcare, it's our original sin.

---

[79] Forbes: Top 10 Quotes From Bill Clinton and President Obama Chat At CGI (09/2013)

"The most interesting anecdote to come out of Federal Reserve Chairman Ben Bernanke's semiannual testimony to Congress: His son, who is in medical school in New York, is likely to rack up $400,000 of student loan debt in the process of getting his degree."[80]

VII.

24.5

The U.S. healthcare "system" is chock-full of numbers. For those of us that track these on a regular basis, they're easy (if not painful) to recite. That ease, in turn, has created a kind of numbing immunity to their enormous significance.

- U.S. National Healthcare Expenditure (NHE) at $3.4 trillion for 2016.

- Growing at a rate of about 4-5% annually through 2024.

- NHE is equal to about 18% of total U.S. GDP.

- Measured as an economic unit, U.S. healthcare is roughly the size of Germany.

- 6 Different studies concluding that wasteful healthcare spending is a range of 27%—54%.

- U.S. patients that die from preventable medical errors each year—210,000 to 444,000.

- About 30 Million Americans (post Obamacare) remain without healthcare insurance.

- Another 30 million Americans who are considered "underinsured" for a major illness.

---

[80] WSJ: Student Loan Debt Hits Home for Bernanke (02/2012)

- Roughly 5 million kids (under age 18) without health insurance (including dental).

- Medical expenses remain the leading cause of personal bankruptcy in the U.S.[81]

That last one is always disputed, but a recent report by the Consumer Financial Protection Bureau (December 2014) offered this sober assessment:

> *"Roughly half of all collections tradelines that appear on [consumer] credit reports are reported by debt collectors seeking to collect on medical bills claimed to be owed to hospitals and other medical providers. These medical debt collections tradelines affect the credit reports of nearly one-fifth of all consumers in the credit reporting system. Medical collections tradelines account for over half (52.1 percent) of all collections tradelines with an identifiable creditor or provider."[82]*

As important as all of these numbers are, however, they are trumped in significance by one that is far more critical in terms of understanding both the shocking collection of statistics above—and then, more importantly, how we reverse the curse.

That number is 24.5. The small size of this one number masks its enormous and strategic importance.

According to the Kaiser Family Foundation (related but unaffiliated with Kaiser Permanente), 24.5 is the average number of physicians per 10,000 people here in the U.S. This statistical average has a wide variance around the world, but the enormous imbalance isn't unique to the U.S., it's a global phenomenon as well. [83]

---

[81] nerdwallet: NerdWallet Health Finds Medical Bankruptcy Accounts for Majority of Personal Bankruptcies (03/2014)

[82] CFPB: Consumer credit reports: A study of medical and non-medical collections (12/2014)

[83] Kaiser Family Foundation: Physicians per 10,000 population (map)

Countries like Germany, Spain, Italy, Norway, and Sweden are in the next range higher: 38.9 to 51.0. Surprisingly, there are only about three countries in the highest range: Cuba (67.2), Monaco (70.6), and Niue (60.0).

The significance of this number is important because it's foundational to every healthcare system. The enormous imbalance between supply and demand can only be accommodated in two ways. Either by an entity that dictates pricing (like a single-payer system), or through a system—like ours—that's based on free-market principles. The trouble with free-market principles in the case of healthcare is that there is no cap or limit to pricing in a system where demand will always exceed supply by a wide margin.

If we could wave a magic wand and double 24.5 overnight, it would still be less than fifty physicians for 10,000 Americans. Given that it takes about ten years of formal training (with residency) to become a doctor, it's easy to see that the process of delivering trained providers at scale is long and requires strategic thinking when it comes to an entire population.

While the U.S. isn't unique in how medical training is designed, like many other aspects of our system, we've sufficiently "gamified" the training to ensure that it too is optimized for revenue and profits. It all starts with the process of loading up med students with the one thing that ensures allegiance to high prices for their services in the future: massive student debt.

Not surprisingly, the financial burden on med students has reached its own level of saturation.

> *"The next generation of U.S. physicians is being saddled with record debt amid a looming shortage of doctors needed to cope with a rising elderly population. The burgeoning debt burden may be turning students away from primary care, which pays about $200,000 a year, toward more lucrative specialties and scaring off low-income and minority students fearful of taking on big loans."*[84]

---

[84] Bloomberg: Medical School at $278,000 Means Even Bernanke Son Has Debt (04/2013)

According to the Association of American Medical Colleges (as reported by Bloomberg[85]), the median four-year cost to attend medical school—which includes outlays like living expenses and books—for the class of 2013 is $278,455 at private schools and $207,868 at public schools.

The saturation is evident in surprising—but very human ways. Westby G. Fisher, MD (Dr. Wes as he is known online) writes a popular blog from that perspective as a practicing clinician and recently penned a critique that resonated with his audience. *[Excerpt edited for brevity only]*

> *Medical school costs and the costs of educating America's physicians is in its bubble stage, about to pop. Our finest medical students are accruing huge debts and no one cares. After all, these young doctors were the lucky ones, right? Smart, social, good interpersonal skills, hard-working, driven, and most of all, disciplined. Look how lucky they are!*
>
> *But when these young doctors look at their first salaries, reality will hit hard. They will realize the next mountain they will have to climb (as if medical school wasn't enough). Tough choices will have to be made. Needless to say, the picture for lower-paid specialties in medicine is particularly grim, yet the reality of fewer residency slots also exists. Depression, already a problem, is likely to increase.*
>
> *In the past five years, the world of medicine has forever changed for everyone, except medical schools it seems. Their costs and expectations for revenue continue to exceed inflation by a large margin. When will it stop? For our newest trained doctors increasingly saddled with nearly insurmountable debt, the lure of medicine is waning. For those already in the pipeline, the reality of what's coming when the loan bills come due is inevitably going to be turning our best new hope for medicine's future away unless the cost problem is fixed soon.[86]*

[85] Bloomberg: Medical School at $278,000 Means Even Bernanke Son Has Debt (04/2013)

[86] DrWes Blog: For Medical Students, It Seems Nothing's Changed (01/2014)

The first response to Dr. Wes was from a 3rd year med student who gave this anonymous assessment.

> *Third year student, already over 300K in debt, will hit lifetime Stafford amount next year which means most of 4th year will be grad plus loans at higher rates. Nothing is subsidized for grad students anymore so the debt grows exponentially. My spouse is also in medicine, and while in a little better shape than I, in a year and a half we will begin life making a combined ~100K with ~500K in debt before we've bought a house, had a kid, put a dime towards retirement, or traded in our POS cars. My family and friends already assume we're rich, and if they have anything at all to say about finances and medicine, it's that doctors make too much money.*
>
> *Treated like scum for years of training, put life on hold for 10 years, and at the end of it spend half your day documenting complete garbage and being told how you will and will not practice by people who have no idea what they're talking about. The sad but true reality for me is if I could go back and do it again, I wouldn't go into medicine. I still love the patients and the puzzles, but on the whole it's becoming a tough sell. Hopefully it seems worth it when all is said and done, but hard to see the light at the end of the tunnel right now.*
>
> *And you are correct, nobody at all cares.*

Anonymous replies are suspect, of course, but sometimes they can offer an insight that really does transcend their anonymity. Some will argue the reply to Dr. Wes is a fake. I doubt it.

The challenge – and threat – is squarely aimed at the very entrance to healthcare services – primary care. Why? The calculus that Dr. Wes referenced is very real. With the amount of student debt – and shortened earning power (about 10 years) – the options for a reasonably comfortable way of life are being continually squeezed into a narrow band of high-paying sub-specialties.

Every spring, an online publication known as Medscape (owned by WebMD) publishes the average annual physician compensation by specialty for the previous year. Here's the one for 2014 (published in 2015).[87]

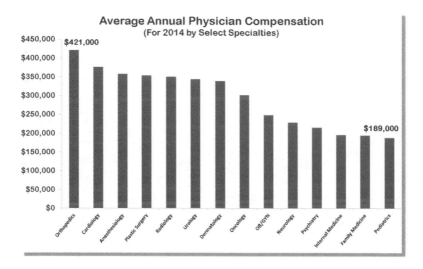

At the time of graduation, the financial calculus becomes pretty basic and reduced to easy spreadsheet math. How long will it take a medical student (with an average amount of student debt) to become debt free? While it's not a straight calculation (specialists typically require even more training), it's easy to see the choices around graduation. Using a five-year timeline at 6% interest, it would take over $4,000 per month to retire 4 years of debt accrued at public medical school. So, just what percentage of income does that payment represent at opposite ends of the Medscape compensation spectrum?

- For an orthopedic specialist: $4,000 = 11% of average monthly income ($35,000)

- For a primary care physician: $4,000 = 25% of average monthly income ($15,800)

[87] Medscape - Physician Compensation Report 2015

This is crude math, of course, but beyond the straight calculation is the growing frustration around the lack of autonomy. The appeal for autonomy is also what drives many physicians into small or even solo practices. The challenge here is all the overhead of running a small business—combined with student, mortgage and car debt—all while running the business profitably. The demand for more patients as the primary mechanism for more revenue began years ago. The only relief for many is to sell the practice to a larger entity and become a small, salaried cog in a bigger wheel.

That's the internal calculus. It's relatively easy to see—and understand. The external one—the one to the system as a whole—is even more dire and growing worse. It translates directly to a shortfall in the number of available physicians in the future. In effect, there is significant and growing downward pressure on that 24.5 figure at the exact time that the country is growing in size and aging rapidly. About 10,000 Americans turn 65 every day—and will for each of the next 14 years.

A report commissioned by the Association of American Medical Colleges (released in March of 2015[88]) summarized the situation this way.

> *Demand for physicians continues to grow faster than supply, leading to a projected shortfall of between 46,100 and 90,400 physicians by 2025.*

> *Projected shortfalls in primary care will range between 12,500 and 31,100 physicians by 2025, while demand for non-primary care physicians will exceed supply by 28,200 to 63,700 physicians.*

For those tracking the effect of new demand through Obamacare coverage, the report offered this assessment.

> *Expanded medical coverage achieved under ACA once fully implemented will likely increase demand by about 16,000 to 17,000 physicians (2.0%) over the increased demand resulting from changing demographics.*

---

[88] AAMC: The Complexities of Physician Supply and Demand: Projections from 2013 to 2025 (03/2015)

Other countries have shortfalls as well, but they've approached the training dilemma differently. Some countries like France support a system where medical training is entirely free (to those who qualify). Other countries heavily subsidize medical training so that the burden at graduation isn't as significant or long.

The argument for bringing free medical training to the U.S. was made forcefully by Peter Bach and Robert Kocher in a New York Times Op-ed in 2011.

> *"Making medical school free would relieve doctors of the burden of student debt and gradually shift the work force away from specialties and toward primary care. It would also attract college graduates who are discouraged from going to medical school by the costly tuition."*

> *"We estimate that we can make medical school free for roughly $2.5 billion per year — about one-thousandth of what we spend on health care in the United States each year. What's more, we can offset most if not all of the cost of medical school without the government's help by charging doctors for specialty training."*[89]

There is, of course, an opposing view and ironically, this one just happened to come by way of that same Dr. Wes from earlier in this chapter.

> *"When a doctor has little monetary skin in the game, how will such a system assure an adequate work ethic from doctors going forward?"*[90]

The phrase "skin in the game" is an interesting one to use in this exact context because it's shorthand for gaming. The real reference is to the amount of "skin" or financial risk that one has invested in a given enterprise—just like gambling. It also crudely suggests that the only true mechanism we have to influence human behavior is a purely monetary one.

Sadly, this phrase has also started to leak into the dialog about patient motivations as well. It's fairly juvenile because it perpetuates the myth that everything can and should be reduced to a monetary motivation and by

---

[89] The New York Times Op-ed: Why Medical School Should Be Free (05/2011)

[90] Dr. Wes Blog: The Unintended Consequences of Free Medical School (05/2011)

extension systems need to be "gamed" in order to have a desired effect. Of course it's not coincidental that by gamifying a system, it's also easier to optimize it for profits. We'd all love to shop freely at Nordstrom for clothes—or Mayo for our healthcare—but who can really afford to?

Any change to medical training should really be architected around those on the very front lines of trying to save our lives. They don't always succeed and I am openly critical of the system they are forced to grapple with daily, but the risk is very real—and it's this; if we're not careful on this exact issue, we'll turn around one day and the doctors providing our care just won't be there. Whatever else we can or can't afford in our healthcare system, we really can't afford to let that happen.

Whatever we decide about the future of medical training, we better do it quick and it better be able to address the systemic challenge. The casino of medical training with "skin in the game" has been generating enormous profits for decades and it's having a negative effect with potentially dire consequences on one of the most important numbers in all of healthcare—24.5.

"Mankind must put an end to war before war puts an end to mankind."

John F. Kennedy

VIII.

THE HOLY WARS

Few Americans are aware of the very real holy wars in healthcare, but as patients, we're all direct casualties of these wars. The battle lines were effectively created through a concept introduced by William Kissick in a book called "Medicine's Dilemma's: Infinite Needs versus Finite Resources."[91] He called this concept the "Iron Triangle of Health Care." It's comprised of three competing variables—access, quality and cost. These competing variables play out directly against each of the constituents in a healthcare system:

- Payers (Commercial Insurance Companies or the government via Medicare/Medicaid)

- Providers (Hospitals and Doctors)

- Employers (as brokers for their employees)

- Patients—really all of us

The front line of this Holy War is the most visible and contentious between two of the largest groups: payers and providers. As this primary hostility escalates, another Holy War has emerged for similar economic reasons. This second—and relatively new—battle line is the one between employers and their employees.

The economic nature of the war helps to keep it relatively private, silent and often beyond public view, but the battles often flare up quickly evidenced by the bold headlines. Here's a small sample:

---

[91] Amazon: Medicine's Dilemmas: Infinite Needs versus Finite Resources (1994)

Humana Suddenly Drops Baylor Doctors Out of Network[92]
Houston Chronicle – 8/28/2015

**Doctors, Hospitals Begin Assault On Health Insurers Before
Congress**[93] Forbes – 9/7/2015

Provider-payer battles: Are value-based payments, price transparency to blame?[94] FierceHealthcare – 4/2/2015

Anthem contract at Stanford Hospital ends, putting 10,000 enrollees in limbo[95] San Francisco Business Times – 09/05/2014

The most epic battle of all, however, could well be the Hatfield–McCoy[96]
level feud between Highmark (a Blue Cross Blue Shield payer) and the
University of Pittsburgh Medical Center (the largest hospital system in the
state of Pennsylvania).

When Healthcare Titans Compete – Patients Lose[97] Forbes
– 3/30/2012

Health-Care Rivals Battle For Patients in Pittsburgh[98] The Wall
Street Journal – 3/27/2012

This last headline from The Wall Street Journal began with the patient perspective—representing all of those caught squarely in the middle of these
two healthcare titans on opposing sides of fiscal trench warfare.

---

[92] Houston Chronicle: Humana suddenly drops Baylor doctors out of network
(08/2015)

[93] Forbes: Doctors, Hospitals Begin Assault on Health Insurers Before Congress
(09/2015)

[94] Fierce Healthcare: Provider-payer battles: Are value-based payments, price transparency to blame? (04/2015)

[95] SF Business Times: Anthem contract at Stanford Hospital ends, putting 10,000
enrollees in limbo (09/2014)

[96] Wikipedia.org: Hatfield-McCoy feud

[97] Forbes: When Healthcare Titans Compete - Patients Lose (03/2012)

[98] WSJ: Health-Care Rivals Battle For Patients in Pittsburgh (03/2012)

"Trish Wyckoff is struggling with stage-four breast cancer, but now the 53-year-old Pittsburgh resident has another worry: a possible divorce between the hospital system that is treating her, the University of Pittsburgh Medical Center, and Highmark Inc., the health insurer that pays for her care. If the two companies can't agree, she fears she won't be able to keep seeing the doctors who she believes are keeping her alive. "We are absolutely stuck in the middle," she says. "This is a really scary time."[99]

For those of us outside of Pennsylvania, it's hard to grasp the sheer hate and anger that these two business entities have toward each other. Of course, the battle went to court and the Judge is trying to work a consent decree through an arbitration panel, but the pure animosity remains in strong evidence.

"Both of these entities have a view that there's nothing more important than their dispute with each other. Dragging their feet [in complying with the consent decree] isn't the problem. It's the acrimony between these two that's the problem." **James Donahue**, *Pennsylvania Executive Deputy Attorney General*[100]

Major portions of the heated dispute were finally resolved in November of 2015, but the combatants are still awaiting a state Supreme Court decision for 182,000 seniors with Medicare Advantage plans from Highmark.

In this Holy War for revenue, the fact that patients are consumed in a different battle—often around survival itself—is largely irrelevant. The fiscal war trumps all.

Noted industry observer Paul Keckley recently summarized the combatants with a slightly different, more generous framing. Paul compared the struggling participants to the dynasties on the popular TV series Game of

---

[99] WSJ: Health-Care Rivals Battle For Patients in Pittsburgh (03/2012)

[100] Pittsburgh Post-Gazette: Pennsylvania Official Cites 'Acrimony' In Highmark UPMC Battle (06/2015)

Thrones except that the combatants in our case are on a quest for health-care's Iron Throne. [101]

- *"Physicians believe the healthcare system in the U.S. is the best in world largely due to their prowess, but at risk of losing its preeminence due to unwelcome intrusion from regulators and outsiders who dare challenge medicine's role. They think health plans provide marginal value, add administrative hassle and pay them less each year. They believe the medical profession stands above all others in knowing how best the system should be run, and decry efforts to standardize diagnosis and treatment as cookbook medicine, report cards about physician performance as ill-conceived and inaccurate, and narrowing networks as demonic."*

- *"Health insurers believe the system is fundamentally flawed as a result of its chronic neglect of costs and purposeful lack of transparency about its prices and outcomes. Health plans believe theirs is the mission of care coordination, population health management and cost containment and they discount efforts by physicians and hospitals to attempt any of these in a meaningful, systemic way."*

- *"Hospitals believe physicians are essential to the system's clinical performance and see themselves as the organizer of health services in their communities. They believe health insurers provide nominal value relative for the administrative burden they add and think 'shared savings' is an oxymoron since the most savings aren't shared at all. They believe plan consolidation will increase the advantage they already have in many markets, see the government's effort to reform healthcare via the transition from volume to value as incomplete unless accompanied by solutions to runaway drug costs and increased responsibility for the underinsured and uninsured that use their facilities and leave bills unpaid."*

---

[101] Keckley: Healthcare's Game of Thrones - Paul Keckley (09/2015)

This assessment is fair and clear-eyed, but it belies the oversized egos, the multi-million dollar salaries and the sheer indifference to patient safety.

Paul actually missed a relatively new but significant combatant in this struggle—the employer. While this holy war isn't as large as the payer-provider one—it's the same economic battle over cost. Many of the largest employers are self-insured (and more are joining the ranks as that process becomes viable for even small employers) meaning that they are no longer dependent on large health insurers to make clinical decisions for their employees. In effect, employers are basically the payer and they're more than willing and eager to drive the healthcare spreadsheet on behalf of their employees.

Many employers feel that they've been victimized for too long by greedy 3rd parties that they are forced to negotiate with annually—and who they feel are responsible for the cost chaos.

One writer I know alluded to the battle with a fairly cynical headline.

Patients Are More Than A Vessel For Billing Codes[102]

As highlighted in an earlier chapter (The Original Sin), employers were initially satisfied to simply use health benefits as a weapon in their war for talent, but through the years, it's escalated to a point where at least some employers want to become more active participants in the raging price war. Sometimes the battle is over religious beliefs, as is evident with companies like Hobby Lobby, but mostly it's about money and employers are feeling emboldened by recent court cases that have ruled in their favor.

The most recent example is a relatively small company called Flambeau in Wisconsin. An employee there missed the deadline for a biometric screening test that the company required as a part of their health plan.

---

[102] Techcrunch: Patients Are More Than Just Vessels For Billing Codes (03/2012)

Dale Arnold, who worked for Wisconsin plastics maker Flambeau, chose not to take his work-sponsored health assessment and biometric screening. The company responded by pulling his insurance coverage. According to several federal courts – including one that ruled in favor of Flambeau – this is all perfectly legal.[103]

After losing health coverage, the Equal Employment Opportunity Commission filed a lawsuit on behalf of the employee in September of 2014. In an embarrassing defeat in December of 2015, the court ruled against the E.E.O.C. and in favor of the employer.

In the ruling against the E.E.O.C., the judge in the Federal District Court for the Western District of Wisconsin cited a 2011 decision in Florida, later affirmed by a federal appeals court, that said employers could screen employees for health risks when offering health insurance.[104]

Perhaps the most aggressive example of this new type of emboldened employer is Intel, with over 100,000 employees. The announcement in 2013 didn't capture national attention, but it signaled a new breed of healthcare: focused employer.

Dissatisfied with previous cost and quality efforts, computer chip giant Intel Corp. has entered an unusual direct contract with Presbyterian Healthcare Services for a narrow-network, accountable care-style arrangement for its employees in New Mexico.

The arrangement, which started in January, covers about 5,400 individuals at Intel's manufacturing plant in Rio Rancho, N.M. The California-based software developer and computer chip maker, which is self-insured, decided to contract directly with a single provider system rather than working with a national commercial health insurer this year

---

[103] Bloomberg: Employee Wellness Programs Not So Voluntary Anymore (01/2016)

[104] NYT: Employee Wellness Programs Use Carrots and, Increasingly, Sticks (01/2016)

to administer its benefits for some of its eight health plans options. Intel declined to name the insurer.

The deal offers Intel employees a narrow network of Presbyterian providers as two of four health plan options, which will enable the health system to better manage care, said Tami Graham, Intel's global benefits design manager. Outside the network, Intel employees are "getting care that's not coordinated and may not be in their best interest," she said. Presbyterian's physicians can do more to control costs when patients cannot roam to independent or rival providers. Intel employees who selected Presbyterian's narrow network coverage will pay more for seeking care elsewhere.[105]

Large employers—like Walmart—have already contracted with "Centers of Excellence" for specific healthcare conditions (joint replacements, heart and spine surgeries for example[106]), but Intel is an example of assuming the risk of the entire spectrum of healthcare services.

The risk to this employer–managed healthcare is largely overlooked, or has yet to be challenged legally, but it will be. The questions for HR departments cascade quickly.[107]

1. *Should religion be declared in the hiring process?*

2. *Should employers declare a religion to existing employees and customers?*

3. *Might employer's group insurance rates increase if they decide to deprive female employees of comprehensive reproductive health care?*

4. *Are employers prepared for pregnancy related attrition?*

---

[105] Modern Healthcare: Slimming Options - Intel Adopts Narrow Network To Better Manage Care (07/2013)

[106] Walmart: Walmart Expands Health Benefits to Cover Heart and Spine Surgeries (10/2012)

[107] LinkedIn: Hobby Lobby Alert for Employers by Victoria Pynchon (07/2014)

5.   *Can employers now refuse to hire or serve gays as a higher risk to healthcare costs?*

It's not just nasty HR−related issues either. It goes to the heart of every company's bottom line.

> *Two things that happened in 2012. We had two AOL-ers that had distressed babies that were born that we paid a million dollars each to make sure those babies were OK in general. And those are the things that add up into our benefits cost. So when we had the final decision about what benefits to cut because of the increased healthcare costs, we made the decision, and I made the decision, to basically change the 401(k) plan.[108]*
> **Tim Armstrong** - *AOL CEO in Memo to Employees*

The mother of one of the "distressed babies"—Deanna Fei—went on to write a moving book about the entire experience.

> **Girl In Glass** − How My "Distressed Baby" Defied the Odds, Shamed a CEO, and Taught Me the Essence of Love, Heartbreak, and Miracles[109]

Mark Bertolini—the CEO of Aetna—summarized the challenge of this never-ever ending holy war in a keynote at the large (40,000+ attendees) annual healthcare conference called HIMSS in 2014.

> *"So I want to talk about the infamous iron triangle in healthcare— access, quality and cost. The problem with this thing as you can see is that between consumers and employers it's all about cost and access, between employers and providers it's about quality and cost and between providers and consumers it's about access and quality."*

---

[108] Forbes: Did AOL CEO Tim Armstrong Violate HIPAA? (02/2014)
[109] Deanna Fei website - Girl In Glass

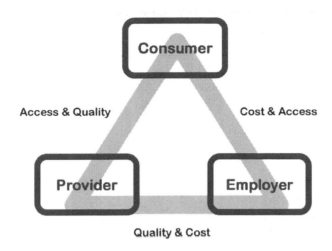

"*How do you solve that problem? And so we've had this delicate balancing act where we first had HMO's when those first came around, and then we blew those up and put in point-of-service plans and then we created PPO's because they provided more access—and we've come full around to the same problem. It's impossible to solve this equation.*"

"*So how should we think about it? Well the way to solve an equation with too many variables is to eliminate some of those variables. So here's my new definition of keep what you have.*"

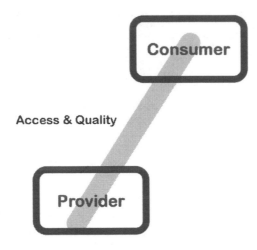

"*It's about the individual and it's their doctor and their hospital. It's not about the employer, it's not about the health plan – it's about this relationship. It's about access and quality – and if we do access and quality right – we'll take care of cost. This is the new model. This is really the only model that works.*"

He's right. It's the only way to end the Holy Wars. Patient safety shouldn't be a part of the economic conflict between providers and employers because it's one that patients will always lose. Like all casinos, the medical industrial complex in this example isn't interested in reason, logic, or even safety. The driving interest by the vast majority inside the medico-industrial complex is the high-stakes game of quarterly revenue for as long as Casino Healthcare is open.

IX.

THE GENETIC LOTTERY

The first and most important healthcare lottery that we all face is the one of genetics. Every patient story is unique and compelling, of course, but this chapter highlights the sheer random nature of life-altering and ending health conditions through the lens of four courageous patients.

The idea of a "patient" versus a "consumer" in healthcare is an important distinction for many reasons, including the intentional and perceptible blurring between these two categories. Many are eager to blur this line even further and while there are new choices today that mirror a consumer shopping experience, much of healthcare—and certainly the more expensive kind—is the result of aging and chronic conditions that can be life-threatening or lifelong. Many of these health conditions aren't choices at all, but clearly the random result of our genetic lottery and why every healthcare system needs to recognize and account for this foundational premise.

Hugo Campos

Hugo's medical odyssey began in September of 2003. He has faithfully kept all of his medical records, so it was easy to share both the written chronology of events and his own vivid memory of what happened.

---

[110] Forbes: Mandatory Genetic Screening By A Government Agency (03/2015)

The first significant document in that medical record collection is a common one called a "discharge instruction" that all patients are given when they are released from a hospital. At least they should be as a part of standard medical protocol. The hospital in Hugo's case was the Alameda County Medical Center – Highland Campus Emergency Department in Oakland, California.

Included on the discharge form was the clinical diagnosis that landed Hugo in the emergency room – "Syncope From Heat." In an effort to help elaborate on that diagnosis, the form went on to describe the condition in more detail.

General Information on FAINTING (VASOVAGAL SYNCOPE)

Vasovagal syncope is a brief loss of consciousness, resulting from a sudden, temporary drop in blood pressure. It usually occurs after being startled or frightened. Some people faint at the sight of blood, when they get shots or when they get very good or very bad news though many other events can occasionally cause it. Vasovagal syncope is the most common cause of what most people know as ordinary "fainting."

On September 13, 2003, Hugo had fainted.

The events leading up to the episode were not that remarkable or unusual, and were largely unrelated to what the discharge instruction described as the usual cause of fainting: "being startled or frightened." Hugo had been neither.

The day was, however, a hot Saturday morning and Hugo was running late to the get to the Fruitvale Bay Area Rapid Transit (BART) station in Oakland, California. The temperature that day was not only unseasonably hot, but it would also go on to set a record for that day in that zip code: 98° Fahrenheit.

Fruitvale is a vibrant, blue-collar community in Oakland, California and the BART station is an easy and popular way to get into San Francisco. During the week, it's packed with commuters and the trains are frequent to accommodate the demand. On the weekends, however, the schedule is a little lighter and trains are typically scheduled a little further apart. If you miss a train on a Saturday, you're in for a twenty-minute wait until the next one.

Hugo's plan was to enjoy his day off with his parents who lived in the Mission District of San Francisco and he was well accustomed to both BART and the lighter weekend schedule.

He arrived at the station late and could see that the train he was hoping to catch was just arriving. Racing to catch it, he arrived at the top of the escalator just as the doors were closing and the train pulled away. It was at that exact moment that his first clue hit. He immediately felt that his heart wasn't slowing down. The rapid beat was constant and the intensity of the beat wasn't diminishing. He had a brief thought that he might actually pass out so he navigated quickly to one of the concrete benches so that he could sit down.

Even sitting didn't provide much relief, however, and a surreal, ominous feeling began to take hold.

The very next image Hugo remembered is feet—several pairs—in shoes, of course, but at a 90° angle to his head. He was staring directly at the shoes of the people now standing around him from his new position flat on the ground. At this point the pain in his chest was unbearable and it was next to impossible to inhale—much like the breathless feeling we've all experienced when the wind is knocked out of us.

He looked at his jeans and couldn't understand why they were so wet. The fabric was glued to his legs as if he'd been swimming in them or running in the rain for an hour. It was all pure sweat.

We didn't have true smartphones in 2003, but we did have cell phones and Hugo quickly called his life partner Paul for help. Paul had just dropped him off less than 5 minutes before so maybe he could make the return trip quickly. Like many healthy people in their 30's, Hugo didn't think to call 911, but someone else had and Paul actually arrived at about the same time as the paramedics.

Later, Paul shared that as he raced to the escalator to get to the BART platform he overheard some people who were talking about the incident. "Someone bit it up there" a passerby said.

Hugo's surreal effect continued with a kind of disconnected fascination for the gurney—which collapsed for loading—and then escalated to a more normal height. The roof of the ambulance had another mesmerizing fascination as it too appeared to rise and fall. Clearly his sensory perception was faulty.

At less than 3 miles away, the ride to the Alameda County Medical Center Highland Campus was brief—probably less than 5 minutes in an ambulance with sirens blaring. At this point, Hugo had regained some normalcy and the ER room process was largely uneventful. There were some tests, questions and forms, but the discharge form was time stamped 12:07pm. The handwritten intake form suggested a triage time of 10:29AM, so the total elapsed time was about 98 minutes.

The medical odyssey to a correct diagnosis and treatment, however, would take a lot longer. That timeline would turn out to be another 4 years from that fateful day in Oakland.

At the second follow-up visit in December of 2003, Hugo was told by his cardiologist to "go on with your life—you're a healthy young man," which Hugo proceeded to do.

A routine follow-up 3 years later with a primary care physician revealed an unusually loud "systolic murmur." That was followed by another visit to a different cardiologist who correctly diagnosed Hugo's cardiac condition. After several cardiac tests, the new cardiologist explained that Hugo did, in fact, have what's known as hypertrophic cardiomyopathy. What he added, however, was a fully dismissive qualifier—"but not the dangerous kind."

Hypertrophic cardiomyopathy (HCM) is a genetic cardiac condition that has a potentially lethal side effect. Left undiagnosed (often) and untreated, the condition can result in sudden cardiac arrest (SCA). The HCM Association estimates that as many as 600,000 people in the U.S. have HCM and it's the most common of all genetic heart conditions. With no gender, age or ethnic bias, HCM is truly an equal opportunity genetic condition.

It's also a challenging one because it's often undiagnosed and it takes the lives of many—often young athletes—in the very prime of life. In 2009, Slate ran an article called **Dying to Play**[111] that argued forcefully for mandatory EKG testing for all athletes here in the U.S.

> *The tragic stories, it seems, keep on coming. A 38-year-old pediatrician and mother collapsed and died while running on a treadmill in Maryland. A 17-year-old Boston boy died suddenly during a pickup basketball game. Last year, National Public Radio compiled a list of professional athletes who suffered sudden cardiac arrests in the last few years, including an Atlanta Hawks center, a Denver Broncos running back, and a Toronto Blue Jays pitcher.*
>
> *Preventing sudden cardiac death in athletes isn't a new challenge. Most doctors worldwide agree on how to do it. And yet authorities such as the American Heart Association have consistently opposed widespread adoption of the measures necessary to combat the problem [mandatory EKG testing]. The fact that Americans continue to accept the preventable sudden deaths of athletes says a lot about our complacent attitude toward the problem. We don't lack good science. We lack the motivation to act on it.*
>
> *The leading cause of sudden death in American athletes is a genetic disorder called hypertrophic cardiomyopathy, which by some estimates affects roughly one in 500 people. Like weeds that overrun an unkempt yard, the heart muscle fibers proliferate rapidly and in a disorganized manner, often leading to a tripling or quadrupling in heart size during adolescence (see a picture here). People with HCM usually have no idea this is happening until they're exercising one day and the electrical system in the heart suddenly fails. The heart takes on the appearance of a*

---

[111] Slate: Dying to Play (02/2009)

bag of worms struggling to get free (a problem called ventricular fibrillation), and cardiac arrest occurs.

The article goes on to highlight Italy—which mandated that all athletes between the ages of 12 and 35 get an EKG test in the 1970's. A follow up study in 2006 concluded that the death rate due to sudden cardiac arrest among Italian athletes had dropped by a stunning 90%. American's could also mandate an EKG test for younger athletes, but we don't.

Hugo was now 3 years into sporadic episodes known as pre or near-syncope. While these were not the full fainting episodes like the one at the Fruitvale BART station, they were always uncomfortable and disconcerting.

One such event in August of 2007 (almost 4 years after the first one), landed Hugo in another ER—and another discharge—only this one was 4 days after the admission. This hospital stay included a full battery of cardiac tests.

At this point, frustrated by a lack of consensus and the revolving door through cardiologist's and ER's, Hugo turned from a somewhat passive, patient into one that became fully engaged. To this day, Hugo believes this decision literally saved his life.

The result of Hugo's decision was a more informed choice of clinical support which included an entirely different cardiologist. Less than 4 months later the new team installed a Medtronic Implantable Cardioverter Defibrillator (ICD) in Hugo's chest and this device actively monitors his heart arrhythmias to this day. The function of the ICD is to avert the pre or near-syncope events that resulted in the trips to the ER—and more importantly—avoids the higher risk of a sudden cardiac arrest altogether.

According to the Sudden Cardiac Arrest Foundation, sudden cardiac arrest (SCA) is a leading cause of death among adults over 40 and causes almost 300,000 deaths in the U.S. alone each year.

In fact, the number of people who die each year from SCA is roughly equivalent to the numbers who die from Alzheimer's disease, assault with firearms, breast cancer, cervical cancer, colorectal cancer, diabetes,

HIV, house fires, motor vehicle accidents, prostate cancer and suicides combined.[112]

Hugo was very, very lucky. His genetic lottery included a potentially-fatal condition, but he survived both a major cardiac event and the resulting four-year medical odyssey through our healthcare system to finally get to the right diagnosis—and successful treatment.

Anna McCollister–Slipp

The day-long healthcare conference was somewhat typical and was streamed live over the internet. The event itself was focused on technology in healthcare, but it also included a keynote by author (and former healthcare journalist) Malcolm Gladwell.

The specific focus of the event was data interoperability (or lack thereof) in healthcare. It's a big challenge throughout healthcare (covered in more depth in a later chapter—Health Data Sudoku) and I was interested to hear about it directly from a patient's point-of-view.

The patient speaking that day was Anna McCollister-Slipp. Her presentation was relatively short, but her poise and confidence was clearly evident. It's the poise and confidence that comes from being a subject matter expert for a disease she's lived with since the age of 18—Type 1 Diabetes.

Founded in 1940, the American Diabetes Association (celebrating its 75th Anniversary this year) seems like a reasonable place to start for information on diabetes, but it's certainly not the only one. The general description—much like a similar one on Mayo's website—sounds official, formal and relatively benign.

Type 1 diabetes, once known as juvenile diabetes or insulin-dependent diabetes, is a chronic condition in which the pancreas produces little or

---

[112] Sudden Cardiac Arrest Foundation website

no insulin, a hormone needed to allow sugar (glucose) to enter cells to produce energy. The far more common type 2 diabetes occurs when the body becomes resistant to insulin or doesn't make enough insulin.

Various factors may contribute to type 1 diabetes, including genetics and exposure to certain viruses. Although type 1 diabetes usually appears during childhood or adolescence, it also can begin in adults.

Despite active research, type 1 diabetes has no cure.[113]

According to JDRF (founded and formerly known as the Juvenile Diabetes Research Foundation), Type 1 Diabetes (abbreviated as T1D) has the following general profile.

- Number of Americans with T1D: as many as 3 million (almost 1% of the total population)

- Number of children diagnosed with T1D in the U.S. each year: more than 15,000

- Number of adults diagnosed with T1D in the U.S. each year: more than 15,000

- Percentage of people in the U.S. living with T1D who are adults: 85%

- Percentage of people in the U.S. living with T1D who are children: 15%

- Increase in prevalence of T1D in people under age 20 from 2001–2009: 23%

- Healthcare costs of T1D in the U.S. each year: $14.9 billion

Diagnosed at 18, Anna now has an array of both prescription and OTC medical devices and apps that she uses to manage her T1D.

Prescription:

- Continuous Glucose Monitor – G4 by Dexcom

---

[113] <u>Mayo Clinic - Type 1 Diabetes</u>

- Insulin Pump – T-Slim by Tandem
- Blood Glucose Meter – One Touch Mini by LifeScan
- Two injector pens to administer non-insulin biologics (Symlin and Victoza) that treat diabetes

Non-prescription:

- Bluetooth digital scale by iHealth, which measures hydration, fat and lean body mass, which helps in assessing measures related to Anna's diabetes-related kidney disease
- Bluetooth blood pressure cuff by iHealth
- Misfit Shine Activity Tracker
- Various iPhone apps

Without being a T1D patient or caregiver it's difficult to understand the complexity of managing a hormone like insulin with such life-and-death precision. Through the years, the clinical community has started to coalesce around the idea that there isn't a single type of T1D (although they're all diagnosed as that), but rather a fairly wide range that requires different degrees of discipline around daily monitoring and management.

Simply put, some forms of T1D are less demanding than others, but they are all potentially fatal. On this theoretical scale, Anna's T1D is at the upper range of being a demanding discipline.

"My blood sugar has always been difficult to control. As the disease has progressed, this issue has grown substantially worse. It's very responsive to stress, which can be anything from a traffic jam to a bad dream, a stressful meeting or deadline. Travel is another big source of stress – even if it's for pleasure."

"Cold and flu season is another annual cycle that adds to the noise. When I'm exposed to cold or flu virus, my blood sugar rises as my immune system kicks in. I may never develop an actual cold or flu, the constant assault adds to some pretty wild glucose swings."

"Lack of sleep is another one. Cortisol is released in response to the lack of sleep and this, in turn, causes insulin resistance in a way that makes it impossible to know how much insulin to take to treat the combined effect."

"Going to the gym and the type of exercise can also impact glucose levels—dramatically—and not just during or after the workout, but for the next 24 hours as the muscles replace depleted glycogen stores. Many people—myself included—get into deep trouble this way by failing to anticipate the overnight effect of exercise on glucose levels while sleeping. I've had many, many dangerous lows as a result."

"Often, the strategies you use to treat the highs can result in rapidly plummeting glucose levels, which can be dangerous. Once the blood sugar drops below a certain point, it can plummet very quickly. When that happens, there is almost always a correspondingly extreme high. So, you go on these roller coaster trips, riding the glucose ups and downs, trying to anticipate what is happening with stress, sleep, exercise, immune response and other hormones that impact glucose levels. There's a constant awareness of your glucose values about 'where' you've been and 'where' your blood sugar is going and what you need to do or avoid to keep out of the danger zones."

"The bottom line is this. It's a ton of math—and constant algorithmic calculations about past, present and future events and their impact on blood sugar for the amount of insulin or carbohydrates needed (or not needed) to maintain the right glucose balance."

As a part of her presentation at the healthcare event in D.C., she described the manual coordination of all the electronic devices and apps she uses to manage her T1D. As amazing as all this technology is, the data is proprietary to each company, so none of the apps or device data can be easily merged or integrated with each other. That makes working with the data— even though it's all available in a digital format—effectively impossible to synchronize or coordinate between devices.

Anna's frustration was clearly palpable and professionally delivered that day and it speaks broadly to the idea that an entire technology community has evolved in the healthcare space completely devoid of national standards like household voltage (110AC) or cellular communications. Verizon and Sprint both understand the importance of a unifying standard so that customers on both cellular networks can communicate with each other seamlessly, and we all benefit from a utility like electricity that's delivered in a standard way (two-prong, 110AC), regardless of location. Medical devices play a critical role in managing life with a disease like T1D, but at least to this point, the manufacturers are free to generate data in whatever format suits their private, commercial interests.

Today, Anna is the Co-Founder of Galileo Analytics—a technology company that makes it easier for more people to access and analyze clinical health data through a dynamic, visual interface. Her technical background and focused commitment to "big data" analytics also makes her a strong advocate for data interoperability more broadly throughout all of healthcare. Like all of those with T1D, however, she's managing a lifelong chronic health condition that's the result of our first healthcare lottery—the one of genetics.

Eric Valor

The story of Eric Valor (pronounced \'vuh-lore\) is both inspirational and cautionary in our genetic lottery of life. The cautionary aspect is simply the fact that we don't often know which illness will strike us—or when. In the strangest possible twist of fate—at the exact moment when his personal, professional and physical lives were at their peak—Eric noticed a problem with his left foot.

As is often the case with physical ailments, this also affected one of his lifelong passions—surfing. At takeoff on his surfboard, Eric's foot would often drag. That created awkward positioning and then falls. After several failed attempts with orthopedic solutions that didn't work he was referred to a neurologist. The exhaustive testing led to the final diagnosis—ALS.

For those who have not heard of ALS, also known as Lou Gehrig's disease, this summary description is both accurate and sobering.

Amyotrophic Lateral Sclerosis (ALS) is commonly known as Lou Gehrig's disease. ALS was recognized as a disease and given the name by French neurologist Jean-Martin Charcot in 1874. There is no known cause and no medical treatment or cure. ALS is a neurodegenerative condition thought to be caused by a breakdown of cellular recycling systems in the neurons of the spinal cord and brain that results in the nervous system slowly losing its ability to carry brain signals to the body's muscular system. Without those signals, a person with ALS (pALS) slowly loses the ability to control voluntary movement of their body, typically over a period of 3 to 5 years.

ALS is a progressive condition that begins with mild weakness either in the hands or the feet, called limb onset, or with a difficulty speaking or swallowing, known as bulbar onset. Rarely, respiratory onset is indicated by difficulty breathing as the first symptom. Whichever symptom is first, most pALS will eventually experience all of them and more. In its later stages, pALS are completely paralyzed and unable to speak, swallow, or breathe on their own. Without technological intervention, ALS is invariably fatal with most affected people dying of respiratory compromise and pneumonia.

ALS is not inherently fatal but death is usually a complication of the diaphragm becoming too weak for the lungs to function. Sensory nervous systems are generally spared as is the autonomic nervous system that controls involuntary muscles such as the heart and digestive system. In rare cases, ALS is accompanied by dementia, but usually pALS remain cognizant and are fully able to feel, see, and hear everything as their body wastes away from lack of use. Movement of the eyes is the only voluntary movement that is usually spared. Only about 5% of pALS have a genetically inherited form of ALS, or familial ALS. The

*other 95% who develop the condition for no known reason are known
as having sporadic ALS.*

*There is no medical treatment or cure for ALS. There is only one FDA
approved drug called Riluzole that makes no significant claim of benefit. The only significant improvement in the quality of life for pALS in
the 140+ years that ALS has been researched has been through the use
of technology. All of the physical symptoms brought on by ALS can be
mitigated through mechanical or computerized devices that can be fully
controlled by even a nearly locked-in individual. Through proper use of
applied technology, ALS is a survivable condition that makes possible an
engaged and productive life.*

*The ALS Residences demonstrate that ALS is not invariably fatal as is
often, and incorrectly, reported. Until medicine proves otherwise technology IS the cure.*[114]

Today, most people would correctly associate ALS with the "ice–bucket"
challenge that went viral in the summer of 2014. Fundraising aside, the
social media sensation did raise much needed awareness for the disease
itself.

*"The awareness level of ALS just went through the charts," President
and CEO [of the ALS Association] Barbara Newhouse told ABC News.
"Prior to the ice bucket challenge, most people – if you said ALS – they
would not have been able to tell you anything about it."*[115]

Here in the U.S., there are about 20,000 to 30,000 people with ALS and
about 5,600 new cases are diagnosed each year. As with all orphan diseases
(basically those with a population of less than 200,000), clinical research has
been slow and there is only one FDA approved (1995) drug called Riluzole.

---

[114] The ALS Residence Initiative website

[115] ABC News - The Man Behind The ALS Ice Bucket Challenge's 'Viral Storm'

Eric was diagnosed with ALS early in 2005. He had just turned 36. From 2005 to 2007 he was able to maintain a relatively normal work life but the march of ALS is relentless and fairly rapid.

In 2007 the cottage by the beach in Santa Cruz where both he and his wife liked to surf had to be replaced by a more functional house inland with no stairs. Since then, ALS followed its typical progression and Eric is now on a ventilator with almost no range of movement or motion.

Undaunted, Eric has followed his technical training and passion which has included hacking the software and hardware components of his life. He has also joined the pioneering ranks of "biohackers" who are eager to test the experimental drugs he and other pALS have researched through the vast array of pharmaceutical filings and clinical publications.

Eric remains very active on most of the social media sites like Quora, Facebook, and Twitter, and he also maintains a blog[116] where he summarized his current activities.

> *"I am now totally paralyzed (quadriplegic) and dependent on a machine for even breath. Everything I had built, bought, saved, or enjoyed in my life was taken from me or consumed by this disease."*

> *"However, I refuse to go away. I am determined to continue to be of service regardless of my disability. To that end:*

> - *I maintain a blog where I analyze research as a service to other Person(s) with ALS (PALS).*
> - *I provide Information Technology advice to PALS to help them transition.*
> - *I am part of a global "family" of PALS formed using social media.*

---

[116] Eric Valor Blog

- *I am an active and aggressive advocate for awareness, creating and distributing multiple PSAs.*

- *I encourage and participate in coverage by regular media.*

- *I consult with non-profit and privately-funded biotechs.*

- *I am a designer of and participant in patient-driven drug trials – (Lithium, UDCA, Sodium Chlorite, Fisetin+DHA).*

- *I co-founded and actively manage two nonprofits dedicated to bringing near-term treatment to patients and bringing new treatments from lab to clinical trial.*

- *I co-founded the patient advocacy group Hope Now for ALS."*

"After more than 150 years, ALS continues to be the best-kept medical secret. With an incidence equivalent to Multiple Sclerosis and a considerably more ghoulish prognosis, it is amazing that more attention is not paid to research."

"For 90% of cases there is no cause. There is no risk factor or lifestyle choice which can avoid it. It can happen to you. With every day of delay people gruesomely die and families are irrevocably shattered. The country has a house on fire and right now we only have a squirt gun with which to douse the flames. We desperately need more funding for research to understand the biology underlying ALS, more government incentive to bring discoveries through translation to human trials, and more rapid access to these prospective treatments. Time is very short for PALS. What if Professor Stephen Hawking had the usual ALS progression and was taken before he could produce his extraordinary work? How many more 'Stephen Hawkings' do we lose every day?"[117]

Of all the known diseases, ALS is among the more challenging in terms of a trajectory and prognosis. Eric correctly asserts that *"there is no risk factor or lifestyle choice which we can avoid."* Only 5% of PALS inherit the illness genetically. The other 95% are "sporadic" with

---

[117] <u>Eric N. Valor - pALS website</u>

no known cause. That makes ALS—like many chronic health conditions—just another tragic example of the genetic lottery of life.

Brooke Hester

At the incredibly young age of 3 1/2, Brooke was diagnosed with stage 4 neuroblastoma—the most common form of childhood cancer. By the time of Brooke's passing in June of 2015, Brooke had spent more than half of her all too brief life fighting this childhood killer.

What's amazing about her story isn't the heroic struggle—although that too is book worthy—as much as her incredible impact at such a young age.

Even with her brief life, there were many examples of Brooke's personal charm and courage. One of these happened on September 13, 2014 at a concert in her home town of Corpus Christi, Texas, and was captured on camera.

The country and western superstar Miranda Lambert was in town and Brooke managed to be in the front row. The four-minute video on YouTube is shaky, and, obviously, the product of a handheld smartphone, but it's been seen more than 2 million times. As the video starts, the band is playing the introduction to Miranda's chart-topping song, "Over You." Miranda starts singing and then strolls down the right hand side of the stage.

About half way through the song, at the chorus break, she then walks across the stage and down the left hand side of the stage. After engaging briefly with a fan she catches a glimpse of Brooke near the front row. As celebrities often do while performing, she bent down and extended her hand to acknowledge a young fan.

What happened next is what caused the YouTube video to go viral. Like other fans who had managed to give Miranda flowers, Brooke managed to give Miranda a small "Blossom" that was Brooke's signature creation—a kind of small greeting card. Miranda graciously accepted the token, but put it down on the stage in order to hold Brooke's hand.[118]

The connection lingered—and by the time Miranda finally stood up, she was visibly moved—literally to tears. The connection was so strong that Miranda couldn't finish singing the song and had to rely on the audience to finish it for her. At times, she holds up the microphone to encourage their help—while wiping the tears away from her face.

What Brooke may not have realized was just how much of another human trait is now a part of her permanent legacy—that of a cancer pioneer. It's not a role that anyone asks for, of course, but like her other attributes—she handled it with grace and courage for more than 1/2 of her life.

According to the CDC, the mortality rate for cancer is second only to heart disease and by 2030 it will become the leading cause of death in the United States.

> "Cancer is a worldwide scourge – the fastest growing disease on earth. By 2030 there will be as many as 22 million cases worldwide. Cancer afflicts 1.7 million Americans each year and kills 600,000 of them. More will die from cancer over the next 2 years than died in combat in all the wars the United States has ever fought – combined."[119]

While the U.S. healthcare system lurches and lunges into its sixth year of politically polarizing reform, our decade's long war on cancer had two significant events in 2015—and another one in early 2016.

The first (January, 2015) was President Obama's $215 million announcement of the Precision Medicine Initiative.[120] The second (April, 2015) was the six-hour long Ken Burns documentary, Cancer: The Emperor of All

---

[118] YouTube: Miranda Lambert and Brooke Hester at Corpus Christi concert (09/2014)

[119] Forbes: Top 10 Quotes From First Episode of Ken Burns Documentary: 'Emperor of All Maladies' (04/2015)

[120] The White House: The Precision Medicine Initiative (01/2015)

Maladies[121] (which aired commercial free on PBS). The third was President Obama's announcement of a "moonshot" to cure cancer in his last State of the Union address (January, 2016).[122]

While the Ken Burns documentary is largely a biography of cancer, the other two represent National commitments of renewal to our original "war on cancer" which was announced by President Nixon in 1971.

The stories and headlines surrounding precision medicine are often breathless and breathtaking but they also tilt heavily toward the clinical and research communities. The missing element—and the one that changes the whole equation—is always the human one and that's also what makes stories like Brooke's so unique and compelling.

Brooke's cancer also placed her at the very center of an amazing cast of clinical pioneers that are committed to finding a cure for all pediatric cancers. These pioneers also give us new insight into the mechanics of precision medicine and what we can expect in the battles ahead against one of mankind's wiliest of foes.

> *"If you could find one great theme in cancer over the last 100 years – it's the men and women who have said 'I'm not taking this anymore – I'm going to try something else.' And that's how science and medicine are advanced – by people refusing to take the status quo."*[123]

As with all fatal illnesses, however, it's the patients themselves who are the true pioneers'—and exactly why Brooke so clearly represents this new frontier.

---

[121] PBS Video: Cancer - The Emperor of All Maladies (03/2015)

[122] NBC News: Time Is Right for Obama's Ambitious Cancer 'Moonshot,' Experts Say (01/2016)

[123] Forbes: Top 10 Quotes From the 2nd Episode of Ken Burns Documentary: 'Emperor of All Maladies' (04/2015)

"When it comes to health, your zip code matters more than your genetic code."

Dr. Tony Iton – The California Endowment Health Journalism Fellowships 2013[124]

X.

AN OUNCE OF PREVENTION

The argument is compelling. If you can't (or won't) control the supply side of healthcare in a way that dramatically affects cost, simply flip the focus to the demand side. It's an almost limitless opportunity with an endless list of experiments that can be attempted to control unhealthy behavior. The theory here is that these changes will radically influence our bulging cost waistline and improve our health.

But are we just substituting one cost burden for another? Is there a return-on-investment to all the wellness, "digital health" and dietary supplements that are aimed squarely at our waistline? Are they having an impact on our waist or just our wallet?

In general, there are three big industry sectors targeting preventative health and wellness.

1. Workplace "wellness" in the U.S. is a $6B a year industry[125]

2. Venture funding into the "digital health" sector in the U.S. is over $4 billion a year[126]

3. The U.S. market for dietary supplements (all types) is estimated at about $25 billion for 2015[127]

---

[124] Forbes - The Top Ten Healthcare Quotes For 2013 (12/2013)

[125] RAND - Do Workplace Wellness Programs Save Employers Money? (2013)

[126] Rock Health Venture Funding for 2014 and 1H2015 (Fall 2015)

[127] Cashing in on the booming market for dietary supplements - McKinsey & Company (12/2013)

Collectively, these three categories represent over $35 billion— a year. I like to reference them as the breezy, breathless bromides of healthcare because the headlines are often shallow and mind-numbing. They typically start with market sizing or dollars invested as a proxy for any hard scientific evidence. The argument is that investors somehow know the consumer markets better than the scientific community. They often do, of course, but it's the business of revenue extraction so watch your wallet. Any health creation is secondary and accidental—if there's any at all.

This thinking is centralized in sheltered enclaves like Silicon Valley where reality can be easy—and wildly profitable—to distort. Every day another Uber or WhatsApp is being incubated and funded. Lavish rewards are soon to follow as these "unicorns" (startups with a valuation above $1 billion) navigate their Tesla's from the VC's on Sand Hill Road to the paneled boardrooms of Wall Street and then onto the victory lap of ringing the bell at the New York Stock Exchange. Venture investment rounds (literally the "risk capital") are no longer measured in millions, but hundreds of millions of dollars. Several have recently secured "debt financing" in the billions of dollars.

In this rarified air, it's easy to see how the "promise of wellness" fits right in. The focus has shifted from patients with chronic conditions and sickcare to consumers and wellness. There's even a vigorous debate swirling around what to call these life forms—consumers or patients? If we can force the consumer moniker to fit, we can foist all manner of healthcare responsibility—both clinical and financial—onto these poor souls.

Wellness programs themselves were heavily touted and actually endorsed as a part of Obamacare. How that happened is an embarrassing footnote to the President and his signature legislation.

The ball started rolling on the "wellness" parade when the faux-science was trumpeted by Safeway CEO Steven Burd so loudly that it was actually baked into Obamacare. It became known simply as "the Safeway Amendment" to the President's signature legislation.

The idea is to reward employees for "healthy behavior" by charging higher-premiums for lower scores on benchmark health measures like weight, blood pressure and cholesterol tests. The theory espoused by Mr. Burd was that the program at Safeway resulted in both healthier employees and dramatically lower healthcare costs for the company.

Except that it really didn't. The one-year savings that Safeway showcased as a part of their pitch on Capitol Hill turned out to be the result of a larger overhaul of their entire benefits program—and not attributable to any wellness program at all.

The core belief behind the motivation to make people directly accountable for their health was summarized by Ken Shachmut, a Senior Vice President at Safeway.

> *"I have no problem with a smoker having a 10-pack-a-day habit and killing him or herself. I mean, it's a personal choice. It's a free country. I just don't want to have to pay the health-care costs of that personal choice. And the same thing is true for obesity."*[128]

It's a compelling argument until you realize the slippery slope ahead. Smoking is easy to chastise, but what about that Thirsty-Two-Ounce soda being carted into work every morning? Is that another "personal choice" with dire health consequences that deserves a financial punishment through HR? Many people contract lung cancer having never smoked—how should HR treat the entire range of clinical possibilities?

The idea that behavior is easily modifiable with simple economic incentives is a popular one, but one that is unproven relative to any clinical benefit, and has no accounting for the toxic effects of other variables like workplace stress or low-wages heaped on by employers. The addictive properties of sugar, tobacco, and other "lifestyle" choices are well documented—even if they're less well understood.

---

[128] <u>Misleading claims about Safeway wellness incentives shape health-care bill - WaPo</u>

The economic "incentives" are often referred to as the "carrot" because they're designed to reward healthy behavior. The stick, of course, is punishment for "unhealthy" behavior. The popular Silicon Valley attribute to this consumer attention is called affectionately "gamification" and the vehicle is the smartphone. Loaded with sensors and "apps," this easily becomes a kind of portable slot machine of rewards and penalties. Lost is the obvious parallel is the fact that many real lottery applications—the Illinois State Lottery to name but one—is also downloadable.

But there's a problem with gamification and Ian Bogost captured it perfectly with his headline in 2011: **Gamification is Bullshit**. It's a seminal piece that isn't remotely flip or glib. He talks about gamification as it relates to "big business," but the whole concept has been co-opted by "innovators" of all stripes and sizes for all types of marketing purposes—including the marketing of consumer health and wellness.

> *More specifically, gamification is marketing bullshit, invented by consultants as a means to capture the wild, coveted beast that is videogames and to domesticate it for use in the grey, hopeless wasteland of big business, where bullshit already reigns anyway.*
>
> *Bullshitters are many things, but they are not stupid. The rhetorical power of the word "gamification" is enormous, and it does precisely what the bullshitters want: it takes games – a mysterious, magical, powerful medium that has captured the attention of millions of people – and it makes them accessible in the context of contemporary business.*
>
> *Gamification is reassuring. It gives Vice Presidents and Brand Managers comfort: they're doing everything right, and they can do even better by adding "a games strategy" to their existing products, slathering on "gaminess" like aioli on ciabatta at the consultant's indulgent sales lunch.*[129]

Unfortunately, even Safeway CEO Burd couldn't distinguish between the carrot and stick during his celebrity tour before a Senate health committee meeting in June of 2009.

---

[129] Ian Bogost - Gamification is Bullshit (08/2011)

"We structured it as a carrot, but I would quickly tell you that the carrot is nothing more than the mirror image of a stick, and vice versa."[130]

Of course it is.

A large and critical distinction was also absent from the arguments supporting the Safeway Amendment—the enormous difference between disease management and lifestyle management.

The first—disease management—is for activities and processes that companies use for a known health conditions and it's designed to keep employees away from expensive healthcare services like hospital admissions. There's real science around the efficacy here, but trying to force the science into wellness doesn't work. The return-on-investment—or ROI—for disease management is both positive and proven.

The second—lifestyle management—is the wellness variable that's an expensive, optional overlay to disease management. While disease management has a positive ROI, lifestyle management has a decidedly negative one for the employer and vendors who sell this add-on are only too eager to blend and blur the important clinical distinction. There is science behind disease management, but lifestyle management is limited only by the imagination and what an employer can afford.

The RAND Corporation summarized their findings in a study they published in January of 2014.

*"Our return-on-investment (ROI) calculations bear this out: Considering the ratio of reductions in health care costs to program costs, including the fees of the program vendors and the cost of screening employees for health risks, the overall ROI was $1.50—that is, a return of $1.50 for every dollar that the employer invested in the program. **But the returns for the individual components differ strikingly: $3.80 for disease***

---

[130] Misleading claims about Safeway wellness incentives shape health-care bill - WaPo (page 3)

management but only $0.50 for lifestyle management for every dollar invested."[131]

That's right—the lifestyle component—where the employer attempts to influence behavior with economic incentives to avoid illness, has a sizable and negative ROI. For every dollar spent on lifestyle management, companies should expect to lose 50% of their investment. On what planet does this make sense? The breezy, breathless bromide planet called "corporate wellness" of course.

This isn't simply a segment of a chapter in one book, it's a whole book— and one of the co-authors of a good one (Surviving Workplace Wellness[132]) offered this summary based on his considerable research.

> *"No aspect of healthcare reform was more deceptive and a bigger debacle than workplace wellness. From the disingenuous cheerleading of the business community to the greed of the medical care industry to the lies uttered from the Oval Office, nothing has done more to damage employee morale, spend money wastefully, and perpetuate the mythology that health is a product of more medical care."* **Vik Khanna** – Co-Author of Surviving Workplace Wellness[133]

This brings us to the second category of prevention—venture capital funding. Here the capital risks are direct and largely transparent. As highlighted in another chapter (The Disruption That Wasn't), early stage investors in "digital health" have a limited appetite for the sector overall. What appetite there is tends to track heavily toward the life sciences sector and the investments wind up looking more like bio-medical research and development.

The profile and trajectory here is much different than consumer facing apps like Uber and Airbnb—although they all have regulatory hurdles to overcome. The difference in healthcare is that at least some of the regulatory

---

[131] Do Workplace Wellness Programs Save Employers Money? RAND Corp - January, 2014

[132] Surviving Workplace Wellness - Amazon

[133] They Said What? Because The Wellness Industry's Pants Are On Fire

hurdles—like those at the FDA and FTC—are designed around consumer safety and not designed simply to protect the large revenue streams generated by taxis and hotels for local municipalities.

The reality of early stage venture investing in healthcare is mirrored across multiple vectors. Big, successful venture capitalists display limited interest in healthcare until it can demonstrate the relatively quick and massive returns that they are now accustomed to. This new scale (and rapid timeline) is integral to their "investment thesis."

There are some early stage ventures in healthcare, of course, and some of these have captured enormous rounds of both funding and controversy. Among the more notable are the blood testing company known as Theranos and the personal genomics company called 23andMe.

Both are trying to "disrupt" the consumer healthcare sector with limited scientific evidence—and both have come under the wrath of the FDA (for entirely separate but similar reasons—scientifically proven accuracy).

Other healthcare ventures with eager investors include scheduling service ZocDoc (which looks very similar to an earlier consumer success—OpenTable), and Oscar Health. Investors are attracted by the prospect of windfall profits—if only the regulatory clouds around consumer safety can be pried apart.

Given the enormous market imbalances in healthcare (where 3rd party payment is largely a necessity), making money—and lots of it—can be a relatively easy process in healthcare. How that translates to consumers in the form of lower costs has been non-existent. In that sense, venture investing in healthcare isn't that disruptive at all. It's simply the same old money-making wine in a new bottle with a different label.

Another popular category among venture investors is known as "wearables." Here the whole fitness industry was buoyed by the successful IPO of an early entrant—FitBit—now the darling of an entire industry largely revolving around the self-tracking of the self-obsessed. At this point, the devices are popular among the digerati, of course, but mostly they're a novelty fashion statement or accessory. Venerable analyst firm Gartner recently summarized their clinical usability and value.

> *"Seismic shifts in this market will not happen until the pharmaceutical lobby has confidence in the underlying systems supporting wearables, and that means that clinical validation expertise for wearables must improve. Right now, the big IT consultant firms barely understand the clinical domain, let alone the clinical wearable domain, which will be even more specialized. Tech startup and niche technology players will play a role with unique and sometimes disruptive advances, but they are too small to provide the necessary confidence to the larger pharma."*[134]

This brings us to the last of our preventative healthcare trifecta—dietary supplements. I don't actually have much insight here and I'm not a good cheerleader for their added expense (which isn't trivial), but as long as they're safe, who am I to object? If people want to ingest supplements, vitamins and juices with scant or squishy scientific evidence, why should anyone care?

I can only offer this opening paragraph from a recent article.

> *In the largely unregulated world of dietary supplements, it's like the Wild West. Dramatic claims abound, most of them unsupported by evidence, and it's hard to know if any of them can be trusted. Supplement manufacturers claim their products cure cancer, Alzheimer's disease, arthritis, and more. They promise miraculous weight loss results, nebulous "boosting" of your immune system, and anti-aging benefits.*
>
> *Once in a while, though, they get caught. This week the U.S. cracked down hard on several of the more egregious offenders, announcing indictments against half a dozen supplement makers, including criminal charges against one.*[135]

---

[134] Gartner Analyst: Healthcare Isn't Ready for Wearables Just Yet - mHealth Intelligence

[135] Another Really Bad Week For The Supplements Industry, Including Criminal Charges - November 23, 2015

The line between patient and consumer is blurring and certainly the allure of controlling behavior in a way that influences health and healthcare spending is appealing. In an industry running at more than $3 trillion annually, the potential dollars are enormous. There is, however, considerable risk in blurring this line without addressing tangential industries that contribute to healthcare costs.

As a country, we've perfected both the art and science of privatizing profits with the hope (and prayer) that we can easily socialize the consequences. There are at least half a dozen large industries that highlight the enormous correlation between short-term profits and long-term healthcare costs. Three of the biggest are tobacco, sugar and fast food.

We've made tremendous progress on smoking, but as fate would have it, not everyone who smokes contracts lung cancer and many others who never smoked are stricken with the often deadly disease. About 20% of people who die from lung cancer do not smoke or use other forms of tobacco and if it were tracked separately—lung cancer deaths by non-smokers would rank among the top 10 fatal cancers in the U.S.

Yes, we've made progress against smoking, but as data from the national polling organization known as Gallup suggests, it's taken about 40 years to cut the number of smokers in half. From a high of about 42% in 1972 to a low of about 19% in 2012, the progress is significant, but that's over the course of more than 40 years—and we're nowhere near 0%.[136]

Obesity rates also have enormous healthcare consequences across all three metrics—disease life, life expectancy and cost. Like the raging war between tobacco companies and consumers—there are two other industries lobbying for big revenue and profits over health; fast food and sugar.

The goals around preventative care, health and longer life are noble, but they also represent direct economic challenges around consumer behavior and choice that's far from simple – even when the pitch is a breezy and breathless bromide. Here are a few examples.

---

[136] Tobacco and Smoking - Historical Trends - Gallup

- As a cardiac surgeon, Dr. Dean Ornish was doing heart bypass surgery on top of bypass surgery and was frustrated by what he could see was the influence of lifestyle on the organ itself. He developed a program—and then did clinical trials that proved his program was more effective at actually reversing heart disease than surgical procedures alone. He spent the next 16 years lobbying congress to get his program approved for Medicare payment. It was finally approved for Medicare reimbursement, but he fought heavily entrenched commercial interests for 16 years. Of course those who lobbied against the scientific evidence were all of those who benefitted financially from simply doing more surgical procedures.

- Companies like LA Fitness, Gold's Gym, and others don't make money from members who actually use their facility. The real money in the business is the sheer volume of subscribers who don't use their facilities at all.

- The world is in the midst of an obesity epidemic, which credible scientific evidence relates to the increased consumption of one substance—sugar.

In the fall of 2013, Credit Suisse released a report on the direct correlation between sugar and health. The report was called **Sugar: Consumption at a Crossroads**[137] and included a sobering list of statistics.

- *The 2012 Global Burden of Disease report highlighted obesity as a more significant health crisis globally than hunger and/or malnourishment.*

- *More than half a billion adults (over age 20) worldwide are obese.*

- *The world average daily intake of sugar and high-fructose corn syrup (HFCS) is now 70 grams, roughly equivalent to seventeen teaspoons.*

---

[137] Sugar: Consumption at a Crossroads - Credit Suisse Report

- *A scientific statement issued by the American Heart Association in 2009 recommends that women take no more than six teaspoons of added sugar a day and men no more than nine.*

- *A single, 12-ounce can of regular soda has about 8 teaspoons of sugar.*

- *38% of U.S. daily diet is sugar (all forms) and 43% of that is from a single product – sweetened beverages.*

While the toxic health effects of sugar are generally understood, there is mounting evidence to suggest that sugar has addictive properties as well.

> *"Sugar may not pose the clear addictive characteristics of illicit drugs such as cocaine and heroin, but to us it does meet the criteria for being a potentially addictive substance."*[138]

As a sub-category of sweetened beverages, the "energy" drink market delivers a compounding effect with another central nervous system stimulant—caffeine. The combination of sugar and caffeine (often served in small sizes to belie their potency) is in many ways a perfectly legal, addictive cocktail. Like any rebellious product, it's targeted directly at the younger, mostly teenage demographic.

The story behind beverage company Monster's high octane success is a good case in point. Simons Chase made a compelling comparison of beverage "innovation" to financial innovations like derivatives.

> *Food undergoes the equivalent of a leveraged recapitalization designed to suit the financial goals of its creator. Consumption of junk food (for example a Twinkie or a sugary drink) is akin to a financial exchange where short-term gains are privatized and long-term costs are socialized in the form of horrific health outcomes. The metabolic donkeys—consumers—pay relatively little money and turn a blind eye to the health*

---

[138] Credit Suisse Research Institute: Sugar - Consumption at a crossroads - pdf (09/2013)

> *consequences of their food choices—instead hoisting the fantastic profits*
> *of companies like Monster and opting for a shortened, diseased life.*[139]

The economic connection to health and the cost of healthcare is unavoidable—and captured even more succinctly by Dr. Ornish.

> *The cheapest calories to buy are the most expensive to our health.*[140]

Since the Credit Suisse report in the fall of 2013, soda consumption is down and declining, but the full gamut of health consequences, including cost, will take much longer to both realize and then recover from.

The maxim that an ounce of prevention is worth a pound of cure has its very roots in healthcare, and while the logic is appealing, the reality of actually influencing health through the gamification of consumer behavior is risky—at best. Gamification of preventative healthcare aimed directly at consumers cannot be surgically isolated from other significant socio-economic factors and profitable industries.

The correlation between health, other industries and socio-economic variables is far more complex—and expensive—than all of the breezy, breathless bromides combined.

---

[139] Simons Chase: 2 Perspectives on Food Innovation - Sodastream vs. Monster Beverage (09/2013)

[140] Dean Ornish, MD – Speaker at The Clinton Health Matters Initiative (01/2013)

Vizzini: *"Inconceivable!"*

Inigo Montoya: *"You keep using that word. I do not think it means what you think it means."*[141]

The Princess Bride

XI.

THE DISRUPTION THAT WASN'T

It's definitely conceivable that we're seeing something similar with the use of the word disruption in healthcare. It's embedded in the title of several books (by noted authors), countless headlines, and now the title of this chapter. But like the character of Inigo Montoya in that charming movie The Princess Bride— I've come to believe the word doesn't mean what we think it means—for some really big reasons.

1. Definition

It's just too easy to assign the word "disruption" to anything new and—at least by all outward appearances—inventive. Uber is a great example. With mega-billions in funding, and a market capitalization now in excess of $60 billion, it's easy to call it "disruptive." But is it? The technology it uses certainly isn't.

I'm not openly critical of the service (as some are), but my experiences were "meh" at best. Yes, it worked and yes it was cheaper, but I wouldn't categorize the experience as remotely revolutionary or "disruptive." Hailing a cab with my phone felt about as revolutionary as checking-in on Foursquare or using Groupon. High novelty factor, but also based on a ton of assumptions around consumer behavior, change and foundational technology like a smartphone.

---

[141] IMDB: The Princess Bride (1987)

I realize that I'm not the target demographic of young, mostly single, urban and hip. We live in the suburbs, own our vehicles, and while I travel frequently, I tend to lean on mass transit or rental cars for most of my life on the road.

But none of that excludes any of us from weighing in on the idea, the crazy valuation, the brand—or its constant claim of disruption. In these matters, we all have some stake, even if that's only an opinion.

First and foremost, what's truly "proprietary and protectable" about Uber? The technology isn't because it's largely a consumer–facing cloud service based on fleet tracking and dispatch. That technology was pioneered by Qualcomm (called Omnitracs[142]) in the late 1980's.

In the first wave of "application service providers," after Omnitracs, another company (@Road) moved the solution to the cloud and targeted smaller fleets of plumbers, exterminators and repair services for most of the major metros here in the U.S. In 2006, navigation pioneer Trimble (market cap of about $9 billion) bought @Road for about $500 million.[143]

The point here is that if either of these companies—Trimble or Qualcomm—wanted to challenge Uber (or Lyft or a half–dozen others), they probably own the patents to do just that. The "technology" that Uber uses is simply a cloud-based version of fleet tracking and dispatch which was tweaked for the smallest possible denomination—a fleet of one. Even if Uber does have patents around single use, they most certainly don't have it for fleet tracking. Which is also why there are many Uber knock-offs (nationally and globally).

That's not to say Uber isn't popular—or that the initial growth and revenue haven't been explosive—they have. Like many services that appear revolutionary (rather than evolutionary), Uber became wildly popular with the Towncar and Taxi crowd in every city where it was available. In

[142] Omnitracs website

[143] Trimble Press Release: Trimble To Acquire @Road (12/2006)

combination, all of these new companies have created a way for anyone with keys to a car to become part of the "gig" economy.

Of course none of this has stymied the launch trajectory of the Uber investment rocket. In just over 6 years, Uber has seen 53 investors pour $8.2 billion of capital into the company through 13 rounds of funding.[144] As of October 2015, the company appears to be raising another $1 billion—which would give the company a valuation (at least on paper) between $60 and $70 billion.[145]

That's a staggering valuation for a company that, at least by some accounts, is hemorrhaging cash.

> "Uber Technologies Inc. is telling prospective investors that it generates $470 million in operating losses on $415 million in revenue, according to a document provided to prospective investors."[146]

That may mean Uber is a great investment scheme (as long as there's an endless supply of investors and fresh funds), but it hardly qualifies as "disruptive." This also sets a new bar for investor expectations relative to other investments that do more than hail a cab.

What's any of this have to do with healthcare? It's been wildly popular—if not outright lucrative—to reference "Uber for healthcare" as a way to capture similar buzz and investor interest in healthcare. As with Uber itself, that doesn't make the technology or service automatically "disruptive" by extension.

2. Training

---

[144] Crunchbase: Uber

[145] The New York Times: Uber Said to Plan Another $1 BIllion in Fund-Raising (10/2015)

[146] Bloomberg: Uber Bonds Term Sheet Reveals $470 Million in Operating Losses (06/2015)

The second reason to question all the "disruption" in healthcare is that as an industry, it's one of the most expensive service industries ever devised. By far the largest and most costly portion of the industry is care delivery by hundreds of thousands of nurses, doctors and allied healthcare professionals.

While motivation is largely born out of compassion to reduce pain and suffering, altruism aside, it's also a very lucrative profession. Of the top ten highest paying professions in the U.S., literally all ten are in healthcare.[147]

As we outlined in an earlier chapter (24.5), it takes about 10 years to train a doc. At graduation, the average medical student debt is about $160,000 (sometimes a lot higher) and they've also sacrificed those 10 years of earning power. If you're one of those fortunate graduates—you're looking at how to pay back what amounts to a home mortgage in the fastest time possible. The idea that these expensive resources—the highest paid of all occupations—are readily available and motivated for lower paying piece-work (the Uber model) isn't just wrong, it's dangerously naïve.

3.   Demand Distribution

Much of the interest, focus, and attention around disrupting healthcare today continues to be on the low-acuity, primary, and preventative sides of the system. That's logical because it's often at the entrance of the healthcare system and if you can't (or won't) change the supply chain, then maybe you can have an impact on the demand side.

The problem is, that's not where the big healthcare expenses are, and it doesn't fundamentally change the system. We've also lost a fair amount of time (through the years) chasing the wrong bad guys—the insurance companies—which we conveniently blamed for much of the medical gluttony of the entire industry. Just like low-acuity healthcare, though, that's not where the big dollars are being spent (and it's certainly not where the big net profits are).

---

[147] Bureau of Labor Statistics: Highest Paying Occupations (2012 data)

Relative to our National Healthcare Expenditure—basically all healthcare spending—the net cost of health insurance is 7%. That's certainly nothing to sneeze at, but if you're trying to "disrupt" a system that's running at $3.4 trillion (this year) the question quickly becomes—is insurance (at 7%) really the best place to start? Even if that percentage was cut in half, it wouldn't have much of an overall impact to the system or all of us as patients/consumers in the form of lower premiums.

4.   Startups as a source of "disruption"

The last and final reason that "disruption" in healthcare isn't likely is related to startups more generally.

In the summer of 2013, Francisco Dao summarized the enormous challenge—which really applies with equal strength to every sector, but perhaps more so to one that is almost entirely based on really (really) expensive services—healthcare.

> "... *changing the world almost always requires massive amounts of money, groundbreaking technology, and a lot of time – three things most startups don't have.*"

> "*Really big paradigm shifting developments are so costly and require such a long term outlook that they **essentially have to be disconnected from the profit requirement**. As such, the only people who can afford to do this kind of work are the research labs of big companies (think Bell Labs in the old days and Google today) and the government. Even startups that raise massive VC rounds don't have resources anywhere close to what Google or the government can provide.*"

> "*For those of you sharpening your anti-government pitchforks, where do you think the Internet came from? The government funded this experiment for decades without any expectation of profit and gave it to private industry for the rest of us to make money with. Everything we've done since then, from Amazon to underwear delivery, stands on the shoulders of profitless government funded research. Creating the Internet was the*

fundamental development that changed the world, not mailing crap in a box."[148]

Unfortunately, the kind of change (dare I say disruption?) needed in healthcare isn't one that startups can deliver and nor should we expect it from them. Certainly not in a heavily regulated industry that's running at 18% of GDP.

That's not to say there won't be spectacular successes—with big valuations, big exits and windfall profits. They will happen with faithful regularity because making money in healthcare is never a big question. The real question for all of us is just when and how these "disruptions" translate into lower premiums and consumer costs? The chart for that (first seen in the earlier chapter The Big Squeeze) is not remotely encouraging for any real "disruption" in healthcare.

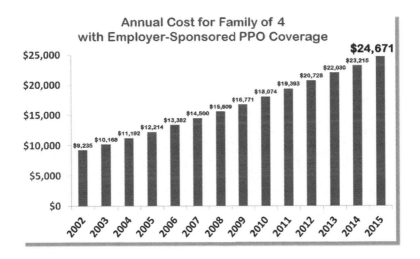

Of course none of this is to say that the venture capital community doesn't announce strong interest in disrupting healthcare with faithful regularity.

---

[148] Pando: Why startups rarely change the world (08/2013)

The best example of this is Bill Gurley—who also happens to be an early investor in Uber.

Bill was in Austin last year and appeared on stage with Malcolm Gladwell at the annual tech festival (and rite of spring) known simply as South by Southwest (SXSW). Malcolm's credentials as a science/healthcare journalist (and now author) are, of course, just as impressive as Bill's are to venture investing. Given this exact pairing, it came as no real surprise when the topic of healthcare appeared so quickly in their hour-long fireside chat. Here's the briefest of summaries relative to their discussion of healthcare.

> **Malcolm**: *"Last time I saw you we talked a lot about healthcare and I thought it would be really fun to start with the question of whether your world - technology world - can help us fix our healthcare problem."*

> **Bill**: *"Yup, I've been involved in a number of companies that have used the resources that Silicon Valley [is] helping create - the smartphone infrastructure, the internet, the cloud - to try and make industries more efficient. Things like OpenTable and Uber that have been successful - and you look at the technology and what's possible and your immediate reaction is - but of course, there must be hundreds and hundreds of opportunities for us to solve the healthcare problem. And so about a year-and-half ago I tweeted, you know, I'd love to roll up my sleeves and see if I can find one of these opportunities and help an entrepreneur in this field and I met with - I don't know - a hundred companies - and I became more and more skeptical as I went through the process. And the real problem is - and I don't think entrepreneurs realize this - but there's an assumption of market forces when you do a startup. Like you expect customers to pay for value and to not pay for bad things - and to want to be more efficient - and the physics are just completely mucked up in the healthcare system. Like those drawings where you can't tell which way is up - and everywhere you turn it's like that."*

Bill went on to describe the HITECH Act[149] (enacted under Title XIII of ARRA in 2009[150]) which was designed to pay doctors and hospitals to implement electronic health record (EHR) software. To date, the government has paid out about $30 billion to all types of healthcare providers under the Act and more "incentive" payments are in the Government pipeline.

> **Bill:** *"Putting [the software] in was Meaningful Use 1 – that's $44,000 – [but] because they're not sure you'll use it – Meaningful Use 2 is proving that you're using the software you put in place in Meaningful Use 1 and that's another $17,000 for the doctor. And it's insane. It's asinine."*

He's definitely not alone in that assessment. One of the Top Ten Healthcare Quotes I suggested for 2014 was this one from Google Co-Founder Sergey Brin:

> *"Generally, health is just so heavily regulated. It's just a painful business to be in. It's just not necessarily how I want to spend my time."*[151]

Veteran venture capitalist and prolific blogger Fred Wilson also wrote about the topic of investing in early stage healthcare ventures in November of 2011.

> *"When we look at healthcare, what's wrong with it, and what needs to happen to fix it, we can't see as clearly how the web, technology, and large networks of engaged users can impact healthcare in a positive way. But that is starting to change. We know that consumers need to take more control of their healthcare choices, their healthcare costs, and their health. And we know the web and large networks of engaged users can help all of that happen. It is likely that we'll be doing more looking*

---

[149] Wikipedia.org: Health Information Technology for Economic and Clinical Health Act

[150] Wikipedia.org: American Recovery and Reinvestment Act of 2009

[151] Khosla Ventures: Fireside chat with Google co-founders, Larry Page and Sergey Brin (07/2014)

and studying and less investing in healthcare for a while (as we did in education)."[152]

Almost then four years later (August of 2015), Fred made a follow-up observation:

> *"I think most everyone realizes that a computer in everyone's pocket (and possibly elsewhere on their bodies) is going to massively impact healthcare over time. But how, when, and why is a lot less obvious to us, and I suspect everyone else. So we are trying to figure it out and sharing that process publicly in the belief that the more eyes and ears on our process the better outcomes for us and everyone else."*[153]

The "public process" Fred references is a website where the joint venture with another venture capital firm (Version One Ventures) outlines their view (in four parts) of "Digital Healthcare." The introduction to the four-part series captures their combined thinking as venture capitalists really well.

> *"We represent two venture capital firms, Union Square Ventures and Version One Ventures that are keenly interested in the healthcare space. While we maintain a traditional market map (i.e. a single Keynote slide collating dozens of company logos squeezed into labeled boxes), we find ourselves with more questions than answers about how the healthcare market will shake out."*

"Keenly interested" and "more questions than answers" is a kind of venture-speak for we're not investing in this sector for the foreseeable future.

All of which ties into the seminal piece written by Silicon Valley icon and venture capital legend, Steve Blank.

> *"If investors have a choice of investing in a blockbuster cancer drug that will pay them nothing for fifteen years or a social media application*

---

[152] AVC: Healthcare (11/2011)

[153] Fred Wilson - AVC: On Digital Health (08/2015)

that can go big in a few years, which do you think they're going to pick?
If you're a VC firm, you're phasing out your life science division. As
investors funding clean tech watch the Chinese dump cheap solar cells
in the U.S. and put U.S. startups out of business, do you think they're
going to continue to fund solar? And as Clean Tech VC's have painfully
learned, trying to scale Clean Tech past demonstration plants to indus-
trial scale takes capital and time past the resources of venture capital. A
new car company? It takes at least a decade and needs at least a billion
dollars. Compared to IOS/Android apps, all that other stuff is hard and
the returns take forever."[154]

The reality of early stage venture investing in healthcare is mirrored across
multiple vectors. Big, successful venture capitalists just aren't interested in
healthcare until it can demonstrate the unicorn-sized returns—like Uber—
that they are now accustomed to. This new scale (and equally rapid timeline) is integral to their "investment thesis." Healthcare just doesn't have the
same unicorn-like trajectory as other industries so the signaling is crystal
clear. The one venture bet that everyone is comfortable making is that an
Uber-like disruption won't be happening in healthcare.

An even larger question hovers around the whole notion of disruption.
Should we even desire or expect disruption in healthcare? Early stage ventures have a history of reckless abandon that's motivated by almost every
characteristic other than the one that's so critical to healthcare—safety.
That's not to say that other industries—airlines for examples—don't have
similar requirements, but then they too are heavily regulated for a reason.

"A pack of attacking startups sounds something like a pack of ravenous
hyenas, but, generally, the rhetoric of disruption—a language of panic,
fear, asymmetry, and disorder—calls on the rhetoric of another kind
of conflict, in which an upstart refuses to play by the established rules
of engagement, and blows things up. Don't think of Toyota taking on
Detroit. Startups are ruthless and leaderless and unrestrained, and they

---

[154] Steve Blank: Why Facebook is Killing Silicon Valley (05/2012)

seem so tiny and powerless, until you realize, but only after its too late, that they're devastatingly dangerous: Bang! Ka-boom!"[155]

Just like startups, however, the kind of change we desperately need in healthcare also has a big source of available investment capital. It just has a different street address. It's not Sand Hill Road, but K Street. In terms of any comparison, it's the difference between grind play on the slot machine (where many can and regularly do hit million dollar jackpots) and the private rooms of Baccarat for the whales that are flown in from around the world on private jets. As long as the whales are making money—Casino Healthcare is open for business.

---

[155] The New Yorker: The Disruption Machine (06/2014)

"[Pharmaceutical] companies currently spend one-third of all sales revenue on marketing their products – roughly twice what they spend on research and development."[156]

XII.

PHARMA POKER

The casino game that the pharmaceutical industry—or big pharma—is playing here is poker and they are trying desperately to hide their winning hand. They want (and need) the whole world to believe that the only reason for astronomically high drug pricing is because of the equally high cost of drug research and development, which, by some accounts, is as high as $2.6 billion and 10 years[157] per novel drug.

Those figures and timelines are definitely sizable and it's easy to use them to justify drug pricing that has no theoretical limit.

> The *"market structure effectively provides no mechanism for price control in oncology other than companies' goodwill and tolerance for adverse publicity."*[158]

That quote by Dr. Steve Harr appeared in The Wall Street Journal in 2007 and now extends well beyond just oncology. In fact, some of the most expensive drugs of all are entirely unrelated to cancer. Among the many financial challenges healthcare encountered in 2015, one of the lowest profile ones was the first ever 7-figure drug.[159]

- Glybera $1.21 million (single dosing)

---

[156] World Health Organization: Pharmaceutical Industry

[157] Tufts Center for the Study of Drug Development: Cost to Develop and Win Market Approval for a New Drug Is $2.6 Billion (11/2014)

[158] WSJ: From Wall Street, a Warning About Cancer Drug Prices (03/2007)

[159] The Motely Fool: The 5 Most Expensive Drugs in the World in 2015 (08/2015)

- Soliris $700,000 per year

- Naglazyme $485,747 per year

- Vimizim $380,000 per year

- Elaprese $375,000 per year

While these are wholesale prices (and Glybera is only currently available in the EU not the US), not one of these drugs is related to cancer.

The mentality of pharma pricing has also shifted from one of pure research and development for new drugs to finding ways to maximize profits on older drugs, many of which are "generic."

The story of Martin Shkreli and Daraprim is a great lens into this latest technique on the part of the industry to maximize revenue.

Daraprim is the trade name of a drug called pyrimethamine (used to treat an infection known as toxoplasmosis). About 60 million Americans carry the parasite known as Toxoplasma with no symptoms, but for those with a weakened immune system (like HIV), the infection can be fatal. The patent on Daraprim expired in 1935 which makes it available to manufacture as a "generic" drug.

There are only about 10,000 prescriptions for Daraprim in the U.S. per year. Given that relatively small volume (combined with low generic pricing of $13.50 a pill), very few generic manufacturers were interested in producing the life-saving drug. So few, in fact, it became the monopoly of a single manufacturer. When Turing Pharmaceutical bought the rights to that manufacturing, they legally became the monopoly owner of a generic drug. Other generic manufacturers could certainly ramp up production to compete, but the costs (and time) would be considerable and they would run the considerable risk of a losing price war with Turing Pharmaceuticals.

In an effort to be even more provocative than when he raised the price of Daraprim by 5,000% (from $13.50 to $750 per pill), Mr Shkreli—a former hedge fund manager-turned-pharma CEO—doubled down on his unbridled capitalism at the annual Forbes Healthcare Summit.

"I probably would have raised the price higher ... is probably what I would have done. I think healthcare prices are inelastic. I could have raised it [Daraprim] higher and made more profit for our shareholders, which is my primary duty – and again – no one wants to say it, no one's proud of it – but you know this is a capitalist society, capitalist system and capitalist rules, and my investors expect me to maximize profits."[160]

A congressional investigation in 2014 found similar pricing anarchy among a broad range of generics. According to the research, from October of 2013 to April of 2014 (a period of 7 months), drug manufacturers reported some staggering increases for generic drugs.[161]

- Doxycycline Hyclate   8,281% (average price increase)

- Albuterol Sulfate   4,014% (average price increase)

- Glycopyrrolate   2,728% (average price increase)

The activity of buying the rights to a generic drug and raising prices dramatically has been a popular trend. Here are some other examples from a Wall Street Journal article in April of 2015.[162]

---

[160] Forbes Healthcare Summit video: Interview with Martin Shkreli (12/2015)

[161] House Investigation of Staggering Price Increases for Generic Drugs (10/2014)

[162] WSJ: Pharmaceutical Companies Buy Rivals' Drugs, Then Jack Up the Prices (04/2015)

	Nitropress	Ofirmev	Isuprel	Vimovo
	(high blood pressure)	(pain)	(heart problems)	(pain)
Pre-acquisition pricing (estimate)	$250	$400	$200	$100
Post-acquisition pricing (estimate)	$806	$1,020	$1,347	$1,678
% Increase **(estimate)**	300%	250%	650%	1,600%

It turns out that Martin Shkreli was simply more brazen and public with his capitalist vigor, but he certainly wasn't the first. Long before Mr. Shkreli, there was J. Michael Pearson.

Formerly a pharma industry consultant with McKinsey and Company, Mr. Pearson is now the Chairman of the Board and CEO of Valeant Pharmaceuticals International Incorporated. Today, Valeant's enormous value has very little to do with expensive and time-consuming R&D around new drug development. In fact, it's quite the opposite.

> *"The chief executive of Laval, Que.-based Valeant has built the entire company on the premise that research is largely a waste of money. His business model, which has turned Valeant into a US$42-billion company: Hunt aggressively for firms with proven products already on the market, (think eye care and skin remedies) and cut costs including most R&D. Under Mr. Pearson, Valeant has done more than 100 deals, including 25 last year alone."*[163]

More broadly, this could well be the toughest balancing act in all of health-care. While technology has enjoyed the enormous benefit of Moore's law,

---

[163] Financial Post: The New Drug Dilemma (06/2014)

the pharmaceutical industry is left with its ugly counterpart—Eroom's
Law (Moore spelled backward).

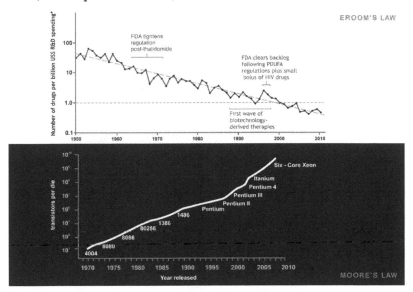

This corollary to Moore's Law is notable because it highlights the amount
of money spent in pharmaceutical research and development compared to
the number of new drugs approved from about 1950 to 2010.

> *"The number of new drugs approved per billion U.S. dollars spent on
> research and development has halved roughly every nine years since
> 1950, falling around 80-fold in inflation-adjusted terms."*[164]

On the one hand, we need the focus (and investment) on miraculous
drugs that cure diseases, and that does happen. When it happens—Jonas
Salk's vaccine for polio and more recently Sovaldi for the Hepatitis-C virus
(HCV) as examples—it is truly spectacular and life altering and the positive
outcomes have miraculous and global benefits. We are literally on the verge
of obliterating the scourge of polio from planet earth. Childhood leuke-
mia—once a guaranteed death sentence—now considered cured.

---

[164] Financial Post: The New Drug Dilemma: Does Big Pharma have a duty to humankind - or it's shareholders? (06/2014)

Sovaldi is considered a cure for HCV—albeit one with an enormous price tag. But even the seemingly exorbitant cost of drugs can be reduced to spreadsheet math. Here's the example using HCV and Sovaldi.

Roughly 40% of all liver transplants are the result of the advanced stages of HCV. In 2014 there were 5,723 liver transplants in the U.S. which were billed at an average cost of $739,100.[165] Back of the envelope math suggests that for less than 1/7th the cost of a liver transplant, you've eliminated the need for a transplant altogether—and, of course, all the pain, suffering and heartache that goes with it. Not just for patients, but for loved ones and for society as a whole. That's an easy and automatic ROI. Even if you need to use long-term financing to fund it—you don't really need a spreadsheet to calculate and see the enormous benefit.

On the other hand, trading the rights to generics like baseball cards and then jacking up the price is simply too easy as a way to appease investors and shareholders quarterly. It's also a legal alternative for another revenue goldmine that the industry would like us to forget—off-label marketing.

Between 2009 and 2015, a host of top brand pharmaceutical companies agreed to pay the Department of Justice over $15 billion for some of their more overt and egregious behavior. Much of this was under the heading of what's known as "off–label drug marketing."

Briefly stated, the off–label marketing of a drug is the act of promoting a drug for a condition or illness for which it was not approved by the FDA. That makes the pharmaceutical companies claim of efficacy equivalent to an elixir or a supplement—or a whim. Companies are free to promote health supplements or "nutraceuticals," and many do (often on late night TV), but marketing drug Y—approved by the FDA as safe and effective for treatment X—for treatment Z (untested by the FDA) is not allowed.

While many drugs have been FDA approved for multiple conditions, the FDA has to approve the safe and effective use for each condition. When

---

[165] Milliman: 2014 U.S. Organ and Tissue Transplant Cost Estimates (12/2014)

pharma companies do promote Drug A for Condition B without FDA approval—it's called off-label marketing.

Of course when the financial consequences are less than the rewards, it doesn't stop the industry from doing it. Over the last six years, as more pharma companies push the boundaries of their marketing prowess, those fines have become significant. The total across twelve companies in that timeframe is over $15 billion.[166]

The industry practice of off-label drug marketing is ongoing (potentially never-ending). There are more cases in the pipeline and more settlements are likely because the legal barriers have no real capacity (despite the fines) to stop the practice. There are no criminal penalties levied against any of the companies or executives, and the cost of the penalties (as large as they are) pale in comparison to the reward. Besides, it's easy to pass the settlement costs on to all of us in the form of higher drug pricing.

Late last year, Steven Brill showcased another egregious example with the drug Risperdal—an antipsychotic drug—marketed by the iconic American brand Johnson & Johnson. While the drug had been FDA approved for schizophrenia, J&J had been marketing it aggressively to children and seniors to alleviate all kinds of behavior disorders.

> *"Over the course of 20 years, Johnson & Johnson created a powerful drug, promoted it illegally to children and the elderly, covered up the side effects and made billions of dollars. This is the inside story."* [167]

Just recently a Federal District court forced the FDA to set a dangerous precedent by allowing a small pharmaceutical company—Amarin—to market one drug for off-label use largely on First Amendment grounds.

> *"The agreement settles a legal case between the agency and the company, Amarin, a small drug maker that sued the F.D.A. last year for the right to promote its only product, Vascepa, to a broader range of*

---

[166] ProPublica: Big Pharma's Big Fines (02/2014)

[167] The Huffington Post: America's Most Admired Lawbreaker

patients. In August, a federal district judge in Manhattan ruled that the F.D.A. could not prohibit Amarin from using truthful information to promote its drug, even for unapproved uses, because doing so would violate the company's right to free speech."[168]

The story behind Sovaldi is the polar opposite. As an outright cure for HCV, here's an actual drug discovery that worked. That makes the economics of the huge pricing (about $84,000 a treatment) at least defensible.

Relative to all healthcare spending (our National Healthcare Expenditure), pharma is only about 11%, but the net profit margins (NPM) are among the highest of all industries.

- Merck & Company   28.25%
- Amgen   25.71%
- Johnson & Johnson   21.96%
- Roche   20.09%
- Novartis   20.00%

By comparison, Apple—one of the most profitable companies ever in the tech sector—has a net profit margin of 21.6%. Several organizations are on record as saying the profit margin for the pharma industry is higher.

"The global pharmaceuticals market is worth US$300 billion a year, a figure expected to rise to US$400 billion within three years. The 10 largest drugs companies control over one-third of this market, several with sales of more than US$10 billion a year and profit margins of about 30%. Six are based in the United States and four in Europe. It is predicted that North and South America, Europe and Japan will continue to account for a full 85% of the global pharmaceuticals market well into the 21st century."[169]

---

[168] New York Times: FDA Deal Allows Amarin to Promote Drug for Off-Label Use (03/2016)

[169] World Health Organization: Pharmaceutical Industry

Another significant public challenge facing pharma is the story of neglect. Here the story isn't about spectacular successes or failures—or even enviable profits. Here it's about those disease risks that pharma actively avoids for lack of profit. Some of these are truly frightening.

One of these appeared with mind-numbing consequences at the start of 1918.

> *The 1918 flu pandemic (January 1918 – December 1920) was an unusually deadly influenza pandemic, the first of the two pandemics involving H1N1 influenza virus. It infected 500 million people across the world, including remote Pacific islands and the Arctic, and killed 50 to 100 million of them – three to five percent of the world's population – making it one of the deadliest natural disasters in human history.*[170]

That was long before there was a pharma "industry," of course, but the one last year—Ebola—was absolutely on their "watch."

The Ebola outbreak in West Africa is believed to have erupted in December of 2013. While the number of people infected (and dying) has largely abated, residual risk is still evident with new cases still appearing in 2016. By last count, there were 28,637 reported cases resulting in 11,315 deaths over the course of less than 24 months.[171]

The land mass of the 3 small countries (Guinea, Sierra Leone and Liberia—where most of the outbreak was centered) is less than 267,000 square miles—combined. That's less than 5% the size of the United States (about 6.115 million square miles).

The story of Ebola's latest outbreak isn't entirely over, and it's a book worthy topic. One possible title for that book could easily be "While Big Pharma Slept" (as an obvious reference to Winston Churchill's 1938 book describing Britain's lack of military preparedness against the looming threat of Nazi Germany). How is that a fair claim? Ebola first appeared in

---

[170] Wikipedia: 1918 Flu Epidemic

[171] The Economist: The Toll Of Tragedy (08/2015)

1976—which effectively gave the industry almost 40 years to develop, manufacture and stockpile a vaccine.

The combination of time and cost for developing vaccines against viruses (and antibiotics against superbugs) is simply not supported by commercial business interests. Lucrative shareholder returns aren't associated with drugs that are used once—often by the least able to afford a high cost.

> *"Commercial vaccine supply is monopolized by four or five mega-companies. Unless there's a big market, it's not worth the while of a mega-company. There was no business case to make an Ebola vaccine for the people who needed it most. First because of the nature of the outbreak; second, the number of people likely to be affected was, until now, thought to be very small; and third, the fact that the people affected are in some of the poorest countries in the world and can't afford to pay for a new vaccine."*[172]

Big pharma's reluctance isn't just with vaccines either. There's a clear and dangerous threat to the overproduction and overuse of antibiotics—which are relatively cheap—and easy to ignore. While pharma has avoided the hard science of vaccine discovery against killers like Ebola, it's also avoided any responsibility associated with antimicrobial resistance (AMR). It's an entirely different threat, but equally large and potentially horrific.

> *"If we fail to act, we are looking at an almost unthinkable scenario where antibiotics no longer work and we are cast back into the dark ages of medicine where treatable infections and injuries will kill once again. With some 25,000 people a year already dying from infections resistant to antibiotic drugs in Europe alone, this is not some distant threat but something happening right now."*[173] **David Cameron** – *British Prime Minister*

The AMR battle is spread more broadly across three fronts; the increase in drug-resistant strains of bacteria, the lack of financial reward to develop

---

[172] New Zealand Herald: 'Big Pharma' slammed for lack of Ebola drug (09/2014)

[173] BBC News: Antibiotic resistance: Cameron Warns of medical 'dark ages'

new antibiotics (where there hasn't been a new class of antibiotic for over 28 years), and the over-use of antibiotics globally.

> *"While viruses may capture more headlines, arguably the greatest risk of hubris to human health comes in the form of antibiotic-resistant bacteria. We live in a bacterial world where we will never be able to stay ahead of the mutation curve. A test of our resilience is how far behind the curve we allow ourselves to fall."*[174]

Antimicrobial resistance represents a truly global threat.

> *"Initial research, looking only at part of the impact of AMR, shows that a continued rise in resistance by 2050 would lead to 10 million people dying every year and a reduction of 2% to 3.5% in Gross Domestic Production. It would cost the world up to 100 trillion USD."*[175]

Clearly vaccine development is different than developing antibiotics, but they both reside squarely under the business and ethical jurisdiction of the pharma industry. One requires active research and development while the other requires careful stewardship by the drug manufacturer. Those are different disciplines—but equally critical and in short supply.

> *"Out of more than fifteen hundred drugs that were approved for sale between 1975 and 2004, just twenty-one targeted tropical diseases or tuberculosis."*[176]

Combined, vaccines and AMR aren't the sexy innovations of "precision medicine" and genetically targeted therapies (with windfall profits), but they demand resources by an industry with the exact skills and knowledge for targeted application.

---

[174] World Economic Forum: The Dangers of Hubris on Human Health - Global Risks 2013

[175] UK Prime Minister Review on AMR: Tackling a crisis for the health and wealth of nations (12/2014)

[176] The New Yorker: In Defense of Philanthrocapitalism (12/2015)

The list of these pharmaceutical marketing and perception "challenges" is long and dangerous.

- The lack of vaccine development in cases like Ebola where the virus is known to be especially deadly (often with a mortality rate of 60% or higher).

- The lack of antibiotic stewardship *and* development (no new class of antibiotic in over 28 years).

- Off-label marketing (Over $15 billion in settlements over 6 years—more pending).

- Direct-to-Consumer marketing (over $4 billion spent in the U.S. alone even though DTC advertising is banned globally except for the U.S. and New Zealand).

- Overt price gouging—even for "generics"—is often unwarranted and can happen overnight.

- $15 million spent in lobbying by the Pharmaceutical Research and Manufacturers Association – PhRMA just for 2015. (9th largest group lobbying).[177]

- Enormous and obvious conflicts of interest that intentionally tilt or cloud research for financial advantage or outright gain.

This last one is yet another book-worthy topic, but the sheer caliber of the editorial criticisms is beyond reproach. The first was by the former Editor in Chief of the prestigious New England Journal of Medicine—Maria Angell, MD—in 2009.

> *"Similar conflicts of interest and biases exist in virtually every field of medicine, particularly those that rely heavily on drugs or devices. It is simply no longer possible to believe much of the clinical research that is published, or to rely on the judgment of trusted physicians or authoritative medical guidelines. I take no pleasure in this conclusion, which I*

---

[177] OpenSecrets.org: Top Spenders 2015 (12/2015)

reached slowly and reluctantly over my two decades as an editor of the
New England Journal of Medicine."[178]

The second criticism was more recent (April, 2015) by Richard Horton, MD, the Editor-in-Chief of the equally prestigious British publication called The Lancet

> *"... much of the scientific literature, perhaps half, may simply be untrue.*
> *The apparent endemicity of bad research behavior is alarming. Afflicted*
> *by studies with small sample sizes, tiny effects, invalid exploratory anal-*
> *yses, and flagrant conflicts of interest, together with an obsession for*
> *pursuing fashionable trends of dubious importance, science has taken*
> *a turn towards darkness. As one participant put it, "poor methods get*
> *results."*[179]

The challenge is real. We need an industry focused on innovation and cures, and while those efforts need to capture outsized returns, there have to be limits to the greed-based pricing. The industry has no incentive to set boundaries voluntarily, so more regulation seems inevitable. That regulation can be intelligent and thoughtfully designed. The best example of this is a project called the Drug Abacus—a kind of interactive calculator for measuring key attributes of value for a variety of drugs.

Developed by Peter Bach, MD at Memorial Sloan Kettering Cancer Center in New York, the project has gained national interest—even though it has yet to be put into actual use. It's a kind of "beta" thinking on how to price drugs based on a range of values and not simply whatever the market will bear.

> *"Right now, manufacturers have total price control, and total con-*
> *trol of prices has led to irrational pricing behaviors. We could have a*

---

[178] The New York Review of Books: Drug Companies & Doctors: A Story of Corruption (01/2009)

[179] The Lancet: Offline: What is medicine's 5 sigma? Richard Horton, MD (pdf 04/2015)

value-driven system for pricing cancer drugs and probably other drugs, and here's a first draft of how to do it." **Peter Bach,** *MD*[180]

Like the other big casinos in healthcare, pharma's just been optimized in every direction for revenue and profits. We can change it, of course. We should change it to focus on truly value-based pricing as well as robust research and development.

Unfortunately, much of what we have is supportive of irrational pricing behaviors that are unsustainable. Whether its people like Martin Shkreli who raise the price of an ancient drug by 5,000% overnight, or the CEO of Pfizer who decides that tax rates are more favorable in Ireland, the message is crystal clear. Unbridled capitalism, revenue and profits trump everything else. Of all the casinos in healthcare, the pharmaceutical industry isn't the largest, but it has some of the highest investor returns and some of the more visibly greedy behavior. As a former hedge-fund manager (now under indictment for securities fraud), Martin Shkreli is the new poster boy for Casino Rx.

---

[180] Wall Street Journal: How Much Should Cancer Drugs Cost? (06/2015)

"Somebody on the Orient Express gets killed (referring to Agatha Christie's mystery – Murder on the Orient Express), and the question is, who killed him? The answer is, everybody on the train killed him. And the answer about who killed healthcare is: the status quo."[181]

XIII.

DEAD LAST

The luxury automaker Cadillac ran a controversial TV ad that first aired during the opening ceremonies of the 2014 Winter Olympics. It was called "Poolside" and featured actor Neal McDonough extolling America's work ethic over other countries—specifically France. Considering the size of the live audience, American braggadocio and bravado was on global display.

"Were we nuts when we pointed to the moon? That's right – we went up there and you know what we got? Bored. So we left. Got a car up there and left the keys in it. You know why? Because we're the only ones going back up there, that's why."[182]

When it comes to healthcare, however, the bravado often comes across looking more like sheer arrogance. A great example of this was included in a performance by comedian Lewis Black in 2007.

"The most important part of travel is when you come home because that's when you see your country with new eyes. I was amazed to realize that we're the only country that tells the rest of the world on a nearly constant basis that we are the greatest country on earth – and that's a little fucking obnoxious."

[181] Forbes: Top 10 Quotes From Harvard's First Forum On Healthcare Innovation - #6 (07/2013)

[182] YouTube: Cadillac 2014 Commercial (02/2014)

"The amazing thing is that there are people who have never left this country who talk about the fact that we're the greatest country on earth. How fucking dumb is that? Because you don't know – if you haven't left here – you don't know. There are countries that may be giving shit away every day. Canada's one of those countries. You know what they give away? Health insurance!"[183]

The arrogance of proclaiming to be the world's best country is really just a mask for how poorly we compare to other industrialized countries on critical infrastructure like healthcare. Compared to ten other industrialized countries, we not only scored dead last for 2014, but we also were dead last for 2010, 2007, 2006, and 2004, as well.

"The United States health care system is the most expensive in the world, but this report and prior editions consistently show the U.S. underperforms relative to other countries on most dimensions of performance. Among the 11 nations studied in this report – Australia, Canada, France, Germany, the Netherlands, New Zealand, Norway, Sweden, Switzerland, the United Kingdom, and the United States – the U.S. ranks last, as it did in the 2010, 2007, 2006, and 2004 editions of Mirror, Mirror. Most troubling, the U.S. fails to achieve better health outcomes than the other countries, and as shown in the earlier editions, the U.S. is last or near last on dimensions of access, efficiency, and equity."[184]

Here's how The Commonwealth Fund ranked the eleven countries used in their comparative analysis:

1. United Kingdom

2. Switzerland

3. Sweden

4. Australia

5. Germany & Netherlands (tied)

---

[183] YouTube: Lewis Black on Broadway (04/2007)

[184] The Commonwealth Fund: Mirror, Mirror On The Wall, 2014 Update (06/2014)

6. New Zealand & Norway (tied)

7. France

8. Canada

9. United States

It's fairly well accepted that the U.S. is the most expensive healthcare system in the world, but many Americans continue to falsely assume that we pay more for healthcare because we get better health (or better health outcomes). The evidence just doesn't support this myth, and the Commonwealth Fund is hardly alone.

The last time the World Health Organization (WHO) ranked healthcare systems (2000), the U.S. came in at number #37. That was just ahead of #38 (Slovenia) and just behind #36 (Costa Rica).[185] The WHO has since abandoned the effort of ranking healthcare systems globally due to cost—which is not trivial when trying to compare 190 countries—but it's only one of many data points.

Another good one is the Organization for Economic Co-operation and Development—or OECD. The U.S. is one of 34 member countries in the organization which was founded in 1960 (with roots even further back to The Marshall Plan at the end of World War II).

The OECD tracks each of the member countries across many different economic metrics including healthcare. Based on 2011 data (latest available across all 34 member countries), here's how the U.S. compares relative to per-capita spending on healthcare and life-expectancy.[186]

---

[185] Wikipedia: World Health Organization ranking of health systems in 2000
[186] OECD Library: Total Expenditure on health per capita (06/2014)

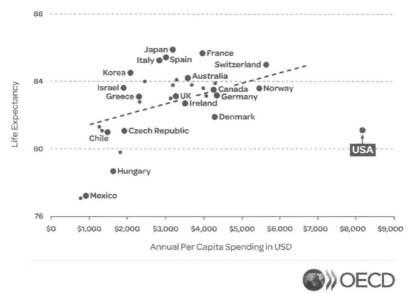

There's more.

In April of 2014, noted Harvard economist David Cutler gave a presentation at an event sponsored by the Brookings Institution. The august title of the event was pitch-perfect for high-powered economists—The Future of U.S. Health Care Spending. There are 101 slides in the compiled deck which is now available for public consumption on the Brookings website. David's presentation (What's Possible in Health Spending) was last (slides #89 to #101). The headline for slide #95 was shocking in its conclusion.[187]

A more efficient delivery system would save 25-50%

The slide header is a great grabber, and not just for what it says, but due to the credentials behind the presentation. Behind the summary assessment of that range (25-50%) are some bellwether accounting firms. The amount

[187] Brookings Institution: The Future of U.S. Health Care Spending (04/2014)

of waste that these six research firms estimated is staggering: from a low of 27% to a high of 54%.

- PriceWaterhouse Coopers (2008: estimated waste: 54%)
- RAND Corporation (2008: estimated waste: 50%)
- McKinsey Global Institute (2008: estimated waste: 31%)
- Institute of Medicine (2012: estimated waste: 30%)
- Berwick & Hackbarth in JAMA (2012: estimated waste: 27%)
- The Network for Excellence in Health Innovation (2008: estimated waste: 27%)

National healthcare spending in the U.S. for 2015 was approximately $3.2 trillion. Using simple, back-of-the-envelope math, the range of dollars wasted is estimated by these credentialed organizations at somewhere between $864 billion and $1.7 trillion—each year.

The most damning report (the Price of Excess, by PriceWaterhouse Coopers) first defined "waste" as "costs that could have been avoided without a negative impact on quality." They then divided waste into three distinct categories, with a range of estimated dollars by each one.[188]

---

[188] pwc: The Price of Excess - PDF/registration required (2008)

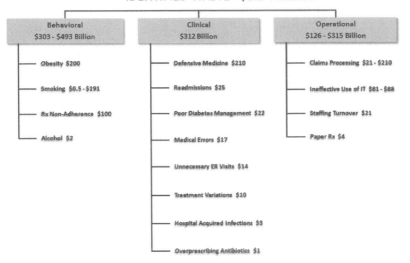

IDENTIFIED WASTE - $1.2 TRILLION

Behavioral $303 - $493 Billion	Clinical $312 Billion	Operational $126 - $315 Billion
Obesity $200	Defensive Medicine $210	Claims Processing $21 - $210
Smoking $0.5 - $191	Readmissions $25	Ineffective Use of IT $81 - $88
Rx Non-Adherence $100	Poor Diabetes Management $22	Staffing Turnover $21
Alcohol $2	Medical Errors $17	Paper Rx $4
	Unnecessary ER Visits $14	
	Treatment Variations $10	
	Hospital Acquired Infections $3	
	Overprescribing Antibiotics $1	

There were some other key takeaways behind just the cost accounting as well.

- 86% of consumers surveyed by HRI agreed that patients going to emergency rooms for non-emergency care drive up healthcare costs. Two-thirds said that they personally had received excessive medical testing.

- When U.S. consumers were asked why they believe the U.S. healthcare system has inefficiencies that have not been resolved, nearly half said "because it is not a priority for the government." More than a third said it was due to the health industry not being willing to change business practices.

- Key barriers to eliminating waste are culture, politics, funding and incentives, and lack of a coordinated focus.

- Solving inefficiencies means developing system-wide incentives to encourage partnerships and networks that work toward shared value.

The PwC report is now about 8 years old, but very little has changed. The Commonwealth Fund ranked the U.S. healthcare system dead last in 2014. PwC had an identical conclusion in 2008.

> *"When compared with five similar industrialized nations, the U.S. ranks at the bottom on all key measures, except for tobacco usage."*

The Cadillac ad is bold and provocative, but it's hard to stomach the sheer arrogance when a key aspect of our infrastructure—healthcare—performs so poorly according to so many reliable and expert sources.

The country that ranked #1 in the Commonwealth Fund report was the U.K. It's an interesting footnote that when the Summer Olympic Games rolled into London in 2012, their National Health Service (NHS) played a proud and prominent role in the opening ceremonies. That's not to say the NHS is perfect, or even that we should adopt the model here in the U.S., but at least one American journalist has used both systems over an extended period of time. His own personal review included this summary assessment:

> *"So my overall impression is that currently, the Brits' complaints that the NHS isn't hitting that 95% mark is akin to saying, 'This Rolls Royce isn't moving fast enough!'"*[189]

---

[189] Business Insider: What it's like when you're an American using Britain's NHS (01/2015)

"This means that any effort to share records between hospitals, or even to access your medical history if you arrive at the ER unconscious, has to begin by solving the high-stakes Sudoku game of figuring out who the hell you are."[190]

XIV.

HEALTH DATA SUDOKU

When you use a plastic card at an ATM machine or point-of-sale (POS) terminal, both sides of that electronic process have been carefully orchestrated to work seamlessly for everyone. The data on the magnetic strip (or chip) of the plastic card has been standardize in a way that an ATM or POS terminal can easily read the data, regardless of the financial institution issuing the card.

Basically, the institutions have agreed to work collaboratively on the back-end to make sure that a purchase transaction can be processed or denied in real time. Sometimes there's a fee for that transaction but mostly it's small and well worth the convenience. This collaboration is effectively invisible and baked into the whole transaction.

These types of seamless electronic communications are sometimes referred to by their unwieldy technology name of "interoperability." It's a painfully long word that's often abbreviated to just "interop." That's how I'll reference it going forward—just interop.

There are dozens of example of this kind of seamless technology interop, of course, in many different industries unrelated to retail purchasing. A more tech-oriented one is the process of creating a document online using Google Docs. Like Microsoft Office, Google Docs allows you to create word, spreadsheet and presentation documents using just a browser. When you create a Google Doc it's perfectly seamless to save that file in a

---

[190] Amazon Books: The Digital Doctor - by Robert Wachter, MD – pg. 189 (04/2015)

format that Microsoft Word (and other applications) can also read and edit. Google and Microsoft are considered competitors but the file format works seamlessly between the two. This is another very basic, but visible and tangible example of interop.

Unfortunately—and largely for competitive reasons—this seamless interop has not happened in healthcare and given the amount of money at stake between very large, competing interests, it's not likely to anytime soon.

Like the example of the retail or ATM transaction earlier, healthcare billing is largely a 3-party (or with employers, 4-party) system in the U.S., but unlike the retail industry, patients are not the primary source of payment. The primary source of payment is the insurance company (either directly or through an employer), so that is how the system processes healthcare transactions. Patients will have a deductible, and possibly a co-pay, but by far the largest portion of the bill is sent directly to the insurance company for payment. The bulk of these bills are sent as electronic transactions, but there are still some claims that arrive daily in paper form. The smaller the office is that generates the bill (think solo practitioner), the more likely it is to process payment using paper invoices and fax machines.

To this point, the billing process to third-party insurers (or payers) has been the real incentive for back-office technology adoption among providers, but this is almost entirely hidden from the patient view. This is also why the patient experience is perpetually stuck in the paper bureaucracy of the 1950s.

To put it bluntly, it costs money to implement technology and there's simply no incentive to invest in a better patient experience for administrative purposes. Unlike other industries, market forces driven by consumers aren't that applicable in healthcare because while patients originate the transactions, they don't really pay them. Insurance companies do.

A great example of this confinement to paper is the ubiquitously annoying transaction called the "patient information form." This one form—with basic demographic and insurance information—is required everywhere, by everyone. It's usually presented to us on a clipboard at each visit, even if the provider is one we've seen before. Why? Because there's so much churn between payers, providers, and patients that it's the one way—and often the only way—to ensure that the back-end payment process won't get challenged or rejected at the time of bill presentment.

That's the easy explanation because it's the billing aspect of each transaction, but why hasn't this been moved into a digital realm? In an attempt to automate, some offices have moved to the Adobe PDF version of a paper form, but even if the blank form can be sent electronically by email, it still requires printing, filling out by hand, and then presenting in paper at the time of the visit.

Why— in 2016—are we still handed the proverbial clipboard and pen with each visit? The first answer is that paper is still the cheapest capture mechanism for most small offices. The second is that healthcare is reluctant to provide direct access to their back–office applications for the purpose of updating demographic information. It's really a security issue and most of those back–office applications are for billing and accounting—not customer or patient service. There are examples where this is starting to change (Kaiser Permanente is a good one and there are others), but actual implementation is moving at a glacial pace.

All of which brings us to the next step in healthcare's technology adoption —the Electronic Health Record—or EHR. Perhaps you've heard this phrase—and perhaps your provider has announced their move into the 21ˢᵗ Century digital world with their implementation of an EHR, but this too has been slow.

Without going into the sordid history here, federal legislation passed in 2009 (known as HITECH) infused healthcare with about $30 billion worth of financial incentives for doctors and hospitals to accelerate the adoption of EHR software. The rich and colorful history of this migration—from paper to EHR—is captured brilliantly in Dr. Robert Wachter's excellent book: The Digital Doctor.

The result of all this tax-payer money was the dramatic acceleration of EHR adoption, but there was some hefty baggage that also came along with the migration.

In general, there are two types of EHR software—ambulatory and acute. Ambulatory EHR software is really designed for small (even solo) medical practices where the majority of patients are "ambulatory" meaning they can walk-in. Acute EHR's are designed more like enterprise software for large clinics and big hospitals.

A comparable example outside of healthcare is the small business that may use QuickBooks for accounting versus the large corporation like Boeing that are likely to use a much larger version of accounting software like Oracle Financials. In both cases, software is designed and sold to handle the accounting of a business, but the two are at opposite ends of the spectrum in terms of both complexity and cost.

In healthcare, this distinction (between a small ambulatory practice and an acute hospital) becomes critical when they try to share information about us as patients. Since one is using a variation of QuickBooks and the other is using industrial strength Oracle Financials, there's no easy way to share accounting information between the two. There's no "interop" and the financial incentives to install EHR software didn't mandate that interop.

The summary assessment of this dilemma was another brilliant capture by Dr. Wachter. In the course of his book, he interviewed the nation's first Healthcare IT "Czar," David Brailer, MD.

> *"I asked Brailer an unfair question: Given his well-known skepticism about too muscular a federal role, if he had still been ONC director in 2008, would he have turned down the $ 30 billion? 'No,' he said with a chuckle, but he would have spent the money on standards, interoperability, a 'Geek Squad' to help with training and implementation, and creating a cloud-based 'medical Internet.' 'I never would have spent money*

on direct subsidies to providers,' he added. 'We've built the Frankenstein I was most afraid of,' he said."[191]

As of the start of 2016, about 95% of hospitals had an EHR system that was certified and qualified for federal incentives under the HIGHTECH Act. The ambulatory side is less encouraging. As of April of 2015, only about 54% of "ambulatory providers" (clinics and small practices) had an EHR. The balance—about 46%—still relies on paper records for their patients even though their billing process for payment is very likely to be electronic.

There are examples of where providers—working with their software vendors—have stitched a "patient–portal" onto their back-office applications, but the primary purpose of those back–office applications remains billing so the function and purpose of the "patient–portal" (if there even is one) is often crude and limited to maintaining demographic information, maybe scheduling appointments and sharing lab information.

This is also where healthcare differs dramatically from other consumer services—either on or offline.

Given the history of paper in healthcare, there are actually two components of sharing patient data that are distinctly different—even if they don't need to be technically. The first is "portability." The second, and more technically challenging, is electronic data interchange—or interop.

In general terms, portability is simply getting an electronic file (like a Microsoft Word file) from one place to another electronically. While that sounds easy (just attach it to an email and send), the sad reality in healthcare is that it's actually more complex in order to ensure that the data transfer is private and secure. Lives and privacy hang in the balance, so security is important. There are fines and penalties for patient data that is mishandled so the tendency has been to err on the side of caution.

Like other parts of healthcare optimized for revenue and profits, however, it also helps that the financial incentives tilt toward keeping patients (and

---

[191] Amazon Books: The Digital Doctor by Robert Wachter, MD – pg. 15 (04/2015)

their data) captive—thereby making it harder for patients to change providers (or hospitals).

The second type of data exchange is beyond portability, it's the actual interop. This is the ability of an application to actually read the data in the file and then manage that data in some way. The easy example from earlier is creating a document in Google Docs and then being able to read and edit that document it in Microsoft Office.

Some (if not all) of the harsh criticism aimed at the healthcare industry for the technical failure of interop is warranted, but at least some of the demanding insistence around interop misses many of the key historical overlaps which I think are worth reviewing—and one in particular.

The first historical overlap happened in the world of packet switching technology and the internet. This hardware-centric world had a similar dilemma during the early days of its evolution as the driving force behind the internet using a very young standard called internet protocol (or IP). As a group, the emerging router and switching vendor's—names like Cisco, 3Par, Juniper, Brocade, Ascend Communications, and Lucent—even truncated the word so that it could become more manageable.

Whether we realize it or not, the router and switching industry—the very backbone of the global internet —have successfully navigated the unknowns of network interop for over 45 years. That world has had its battles and most of those have been successfully navigated or avoided outright. Today, the global internet largely works (and sometimes fails) because of those technical and business settlements.

That's not to say all is perfect harmony or without big glaring challenges, however, and two of the biggest revolve around the vulnerability of seamless and easy interop—security and privacy. Of all the data that's been digitized, our health data has become the single largest target by commercial (and illicit) interests and it's also the richest source of data at scale.

The parallels with what happened in the hardware world of routers and switches are similar to healthcare except for a few key variables—and one in particular. That one is the lack of urgency on the part of hundreds of vendors to act cooperatively for the benefit of both consumers and an entire industry. Given the life–and–death consequence associated with health data interop some consider this to be outright criminal negligence—even if there's no legal basis for prosecution.

Those are serious, some might say exaggerated charges. Legal matters are for the courts to decide, of course, but here are some useful definitions.

Negligence: Failure to act with the prudence that a reasonable person would exercise under the same circumstances.

Criminal negligence: Recklessly acting without reasonable caution and putting another person at risk of injury or death (*or failing to do something with the same consequences*).

In fairness, it's not entirely the fault of vendors who design and sell software. Having worked in the software industry I know that all too often it's the buyers who pay for design specs that protect their financial interests, so it's really a shared culpability.

The challenge to easily share data is compounded by the fact that there are now about 470 vendors that manufacture and sell EHR software.[192]

One way to think of this is to imagine that there are 470 vendors creating word processing software like Microsoft Word, and each of these, in turn, are creating a different file format. The file from one EHR software vendor can't be easily imported into another – and vice versa – by design. It's a relatively easy technical fix—called standards—but private, for profit industries often loathe standards because it then forces them to compete on real innovations beyond simply a proprietary file-format.

I honestly don't believe this practice started with the intent to avoid file or data sharing as much as it was simply easier, faster and certainly cheaper to ship a product without any external dependencies—especially ones that relied on any collaboration with a competitor. Imagine if Microsoft had

---

[192] Chilmark Research: Incentives, Regulations and Consequences (05/2014)

to consult and collaborate with Google before shipping a new version of Office. It simply wouldn't happen.

Today, most of the industry focus for healthcare interop revolves around the lack of HER's to easily share patient data, but that's only part of the whole story. There's also an urgent need for broader healthcare interop that includes medical devices, wearables and other sensors that are destined for our health future. Many of these devices are also hampered by lack of data interop, and in some cases, even direct patient access. In these battles, patients are caught squarely in the middle of competing commercial interests around systems that have been optimized for revenue and profits—not safety and quality. Two examples of this are patients from an earlier chapter (The Genetic Lottery), Hugo Campos and Anna McCollister-Slipp.

In November of 2011, Hugo took to the TEDx stage in Cambridge to share the story of his implantable cardiac defibrillator (ICD).[193]

While the device literally collects every beat of his heart, the manufacturer (Medtronic) considers the digital data "stream" the device generates to be their rightful and legal property. An entirely separate device (used to capture the data for clinical interpretation) is also proprietary to Medtronic as a part of their closed-loop "system." Hugo is the host for their device, but not considered an active participant. In the world of medical devices, the truly antiquated thinking has often been that patient access to this type of clinical data is simply inappropriate and should only be collected and interpreted by clinicians. Using this antiquated logic, why should the format be anything BUT proprietary?

Hugo's story is not unique. Remember Anna McCollister-Slipp from the same chapter? As a Type-1 Diabetic, Anna described her frustration in trying to manage data from four different electronic devices (clinically prescribed) because each of the devices has its own proprietary data formats.

---

[193] YouTube: TEDxCambridge 2011: Fighting for the Right to Open his Heart Data: Hugo Campos (09/2012)

*"These are amazing machines – it's incredible technology – and the care of diabetes has improved dramatically because of them and because of some of the newer insulin's that we have on the market. However, one of the most important things for me and for others like me with Type 1 in terms of managing our disease is understanding [the] patterns and **right now all of my medical devices use different data formats, different data standards [and] they don't communicate."*[194]

As to actual EHR data, Dr. Robert Wachter's book should be required reading (almost a textbook) for everyone in Healthcare Information Technology (HIT) because understanding the history of "wiring healthcare" (his phrase) is critical to understanding many of the current business challenges and tensions—largely around interop.

A key element to the technical challenge of interop—and central to Dr. Wachter's opinion—is the lack of what's called a universal patient identifier.

Using the ATM analogy again, it's as if every hospital, clinic and doctor uses a different credit-card number scheme—usable only in their branded ATM's. You could use a Wells Fargo ATM card in a Wells Fargo ATM, but not in a Bank of America one.

"Underlying many of the discussions regarding personal health records, health exchanges, and interop is the need for a universal patient identifier, and ultimately a universal patient record that would be accessible anywhere to you or others who need it. Congress passed and President Clinton signed a law banning the use of federal funding to create such a number. This means that any effort to share records between hospitals, or even to access your medical history if you arrive at the ER unconscious, has to begin by solving the high-stakes Sudoku game of figuring out who the hell you are."[195]

Unlike financial services, this particular "Sudoku game" is fraught with errors—and clinical risks. In a 2012 Recommendation to Congress, the

---

[194] Forbes: The View Of Digital Health From An 'Engaged Patient'

[195] Amazon Books: The Digital Doctor by Robert Wachter, MD – pg. 189 (04/2015)

Healthcare Information Management Systems Society (HIMSS) cited this sobering statistic:

> *"Patient-data mismatches remain a significant and growing problem. According to industry estimates, **between 8 and 14 percent of medical records include erroneous information tied to an incorrect patient identity.** The result is increased costs estimated at hundreds of millions of dollars per year to correct information. These errors can result in serious risks to patient safety. Mismatches, which already occur at a significant rate within individual institutions and systems will significantly increase when entities communicate among each other via HIE – a Meaningful Use Stage 2 requirement – that may be using different systems, different matching algorithms, and different data dictionaries."*[196]

Dr. Wachter found additional support from Michael Blum (CIO of UCSF Medical Center), who called the congressional ban on establishing a universal patient identifier, *"the biggest single failure in the history of health IT legislation."*[197]

The natural fear—and the one that has derailed all efforts to this point—remains patient privacy. That's not an unreasonable fear because in the course of 2015, the U.S. healthcare system announced the breach of over 112 million records (about 35% of the U.S. population) to cyber theft.

But all this data theft happened **without** a national patient identifier. That's not to say the records would have been safe by simply adding a national patient identifier, but we need more technical security— including an **intelligent identifier**—not just a name, social security number and home address.

The technical reality is that without modern data standards in healthcare, our personal health information is at greater risk as long as we rely on antiquated methods of simple numbers and text fields (that are prone to easy

---

[196] Forbes: Who Stole U.S. Healthcare Interop? (03/2014)

[197] Amazon Books: The Digital Doctor by Robert Wachter, MD – pg. 189 (04/2015)

data entry errors and then require complex games of Sudoku to "figure out who the hell we are").

Until we solve the very first riddle of our identity to the healthcare system, true data interop will remain the chew-toy of large, competing commercial interests. Playing on the fears that we're somehow safer without a national patient identifier is effective marketing on the part of the industry, but it's technically and patently false. We're actually less safe (and less private) using an antiquated, 9-digit numbering system (Social Security) developed in the 1930's.

Mandating a unique—and technically superior—patient identifier may not be the biggest problem in healthcare IT, but it is absolutely the first. Absent this critical standard, we will continue to struggle with competing interests, technical workarounds, faxes and data delivered by hand on paper. EHR vendors will continue to number in the hundreds because migrating from one software solution to another is expensive and time consuming. In the end, data interop in healthcare isn't a business or technical challenge at all. It's really a moral one of the highest priority for the whole industry.

"As a society, we've been engaged not in the reduction of risk, but in the reconfiguration of risk. You don't have to worry about a guy in Romania stealing your credit card, but you have to worry about North Korea coming in and shutting off the power for two weeks." **Malcolm Gladwell** – *The Munk Debates* [198]

XV.

THE CYBER THREAT

Established in 2008, the Munk Debates is an interesting event for thought leaders, politicians and writers of all stripes to weigh-in on leading topics of the day. Held semi-annually in Toronto, the Munk Debates were founded by Peter and Melanie Munk as a charitable initiative associated with the Aurea Foundation. The last Munk Debate was held in November last year and was notable for many reasons—including the fact that the issue of cyber security was not only referenced—it played a pivotal role.

The debate topic for this episode of the Munk Debates was framed as a resolution – literally.

"Be it resolved humankind's best days lie ahead ... Progress."

Debating the resolution were four thought leaders divided equally into teams of two. Arguing in favor of the resolution was noted Harvard Professor, author and cognitive scientist Steven Pinker. Joining Steven in support of the resolution was author, businessman and Conservative member of the House of Lords, Matt Ridley.

Arguing against the resolution was journalist and best-selling author Malcolm Gladwell who was joined by writer, philosopher and television presenter Alain de Botton.

---

[198] Munk Debates - Progress (Nov 2015)

The 90-minute debate can be seen in its entirety on the host website[199] and the cyber security reference was a key element of the argument against the resolution that Malcolm Gladwell presented as a part of his allotted eight-minute opening argument.

> *"I was recently at a conference and I was chatting with some people who were internet security specialists and I asked them "what do you worry about – what's on your mind?" – and they said – well you know we've gotten very good at dealing with the everyday, low–level threats that used to comprise the world of 'hacking.' [Like] the guy from Bulgaria who wants to steal your credit card. There are thousands of those threats and we're doing a good job of keeping them at bay, but what terrifies us is what they called 'digital 911.' Some nation state comes in – hacks their way into the electrical infrastructure of North America and shuts off the power for a week. That terrifies them."*

Under the Department of Homeland Security, the U.S. Government lists 16 distinct categories as Critical Infrastructure.[200] One of the 16 is the Healthcare and Public Health Sector.[201] When there's a regional or national crisis like Hurricane Katrina or 9/11—or a potentially deadly disease outbreak like Ebola—healthcare is truly critical to the safety of all Americans even if it's not all Americans at the exact same time.

As healthcare becomes increasingly digitized (and more medical devices become network attached) it has been under wholesale assault and easily captured my vote as the Top U.S. Healthcare Story for 2014. Here are six compelling reasons why:

1. The SANS–Norse Healthcare Cyberthreat Report[202]

---

[199] Munk Debates - Progress (Nov 2015)

[200] U.S. Department of Homeland Security - Critical Infrastructure

[201] Critical Infrastructure - Healthcare and Public Health Sector

[202] SANS-Norse Healthcare Cyberthreat Report (email registration required)

"This level of compromise and control could easily lead to a wide range of criminal activities that are currently not being detected. For example, hackers can engage in widespread theft of patient information that includes everything from medical conditions to social security numbers to home addresses, and they can even manipulate medical devices used to administer critical care."

2. The breach of the top three medical device manufacturers: Boston Scientific, Medtronic, and St. Jude Medical[203]

"The medical device makers were not aware of the intrusions until federal authorities contacted them, and they have formed task forces to investigate the breach, [an inside source] said."

3. FBI Private Industry Notification (PIN) to the healthcare industry[204]

"The healthcare industry is not as resilient to cyber intrusions compared to the financial and retail sectors, therefore the possibility of increased cyber intrusions is likely," the Federal Bureau of Investigation said in a private notice it has been distributing to healthcare providers, obtained by Reuters.

4. The "hacktivism" cyber attack on Boston Children's Hospital[205]

In April, Boston Children's Hospital was attacked by a "hacker collective" known as Anonymous. While the attack was classified as "hacktivism" (motivations revolved around a high-profile pediatric case) the "group" issued direct threats prior to launching a sizable distributed denial-of-service (DDoS) attack on the hospital. The attack was short lived (about a week) but escalated quickly and did have an impact on critical communications – including email services for the entire hospital. (April, 2014)

---

[203] SFGate - Hackers break into networks of 3 big medical device makers
[204] Reuters: EXCLUSIVE: FBI Warns healthcare sector vulnerable to cyber attacks
[205] Forbes - The Top U.S. Healthcare Story For 2014: Cybersecurity

As noted by Frost & Sullivan (a consulting firm with a cybersecurity practice): "A common response by many administrators to the challenges of DDoS is the belief that their firewall and IPS [intrusion protection services] infrastructure will protect them from attack. Unfortunately, this is not true. Firewalls and IPS devices, while critical to network protection, are not adequate to protect against complex DDoS attacks." [206]

5. Cyber Attack Nets 4.5 Million Records From Large Hospital System (August, 2014) [207]

"In July 2014, Community Health Systems, Inc. (the "Company") confirmed that its computer network was the target of an external, criminal cyber attack that the Company believes occurred in April and June, 2014. The Company and its forensic expert, Mandiant (a FireEye Company), believe the attacker was an "Advanced Persistent Threat" group originating from China who used highly sophisticated malware and technology to attack the Company's systems." SEC Form 8–K as filed by CHS on 8/18/2014 [208] *"Community Health Systems, Inc. is one of the nation's leading operators of general acute care hospitals. The organization's affiliates own, operate or lease 206 hospitals in 29 states with approximately 31,100 licensed beds." Community Health Systems website* [209]

6. The Sony Pictures Entertainment breach, which included detailed and sensitive medical information of employees, spouses, and their dependents. [210]

"Another document leaked in the hack is a spreadsheet from a human resources folder on Sony's servers that includes the birth dates, gender,

---

[206] Frost & Sullivan: Arbor Networks - Meeting Data Center Demands for DDOS Protection

[207] Forbes - Cyberattack nets 4.5 million records from large hospital system

[208] http://www.chs.net/investor-relations/sec-fillings/

[209] Community Health Systems website

[210] Bloomberg Business - Sony Hack Reveals Health Details on Employees, Children

health condition and medical costs for 34 Sony employees, their spouses and children who had very high medical bills. The conditions listed include premature births, cancer, kidney failure and alcoholic liver cirrhosis. The document doesn't include employees' names."

Given the events in 2014, one would have hoped that 2015 might have been better. The evidence suggests that cyber security not only failed to improve, but that it's also gotten worse. In the course of just one year—2015—the top fifteen data breaches in healthcare accounted for over 111 million lost or stolen records. That's effectively more than 35% of the total U.S. population. Four of the top six (with breaches over 1 million records each) are within the family of Blue Cross Blue Shield organizations.

Top 10 Healthcare Data Breaches 2015

Organization	Records Breached	Type of Breach
Anthem.	78,800,000	Hacking / IT Incident
PREMERA	11,000,000	Hacking / IT Incident
Excellus	10,000,000	Hacking / IT Incident
UCLA Health	4,500,000	Hacking / IT Incident
mie	3,900,000	Hacking / IT Incident
CareFirst	1,100,000	Hacking / IT Incident
DMAS	697,586	Hacking / IT Incident
GEORGIA DEPARTMENT OF COMMUNITY HEALTH	557,779	Hacking / IT Incident
BEACON HEALTH SYSTEM	306,789	Hacking / IT Incident
DJO GLOBAL	160,000	Laptop Theft
2015 Total	**111,022,154**	(almost 35% U.S. population)

Combined, these data breaches represent a significant threat to the critical infrastructure of healthcare and the repercussions go well beyond just stolen data.

Self-insured employers often share detailed employee (and dependent) health information with companies they contract with for benefit management and claims processing. Whether a company is self-insured or not is irrelevant. Managing and maintaining PHI greatly expands their responsibility and liability for security compliance, audit, and data breach under

HIPAA, the Federal regulation enacted to protect "personal health information" (PHI).

The full legal liability for loss of PHI under HIPAA is not something that many employers are either familiar with or prepared to defend against.

> *"The plaintiffs are suing Sony on grounds of negligence, invasion of privacy, bailment and violations of multiple California laws that require a corporation to protect the private medical information of its employees and notify them of data breaches in a timely fashion. They're seeking "an award of appropriate relief, including actual damages, restitution, disgorgement, and statutory damages."* [211]

Credit cards have a relatively short usable life after theft and a typically small personal liability—often only $50 to the consumer. This is also why the courts often frown on consumer lawsuits for financial identity theft. Medical identity theft, however, is vastly different and the courts will review these class-action employee/employer cases very closely.

Beyond the legal liability is the larger issue for all of cybersecurity—trust. Earlier this year the French telecom conglomerate Orange did a study (The Future of Digital Trust[212]) that produced these results.

1. 78% of consumers state that it is hard to trust companies when it comes to the way they use consumer personal data.

2. 70% agree that there are few or no trusted ways to find out about personal data management and protection online.

3. 78% feel that service providers hold too much information about consumer behavior and preferences.

---

[211] USA Today - Sony hit with fourth class-action lawsuit

[212] Loudhouse / Orange - The Future of Digital Trust

In this new age of hacktivism, massive health data breaches and global cyber threats, privacy may well be dead (as some are quick to suggest dismissively), but trust most certainly isn't.

> *"As I've said in these memos for more than 25 years, we can afford to lose money – even a lot of money. But we can't afford to lose reputation – even a shred of reputation."* **Warren Buffet** [213]

As we "reconfigure" our online risk (that wonderful phrase coined by Malcolm Gladwell), the continuing erosion of trust has broad and seismic implications, especially in healthcare.

> *"While cyberspace has proved largely resilient to attacks and other disruptions so far, its underlying dynamic has always been such that attackers have an easier time than defenders. There are reasons to believe that resilience is gradually being undermined, allowing this dynamic of vulnerability to become more impactful."*

> *"First, the growth of the "Internet of Things" means that ever more devices are being connected online, touching many more parts of life and widening both the potential entry points for and impacts of disruption. Second, there is ever-deepening complexity of interactions among the many aspects of life that are dependent on connected devices, making those impacts potentially harder to predict."*

> *"While it is possible for the balance of advantage between attackers and defenders to flip, it is also possible for it to become more pronounced. A future in which attackers – whether hackers, organized-crime groups or national militaries – have an overwhelming, dominant and lasting advantage over defenders could be just one disruptive technology away."*

> *"Attackers in this future could achieve a wide range of effects with little input, making large-scale, Internet-wide disruptions easy and common. The Internet would cease to be a trusted medium for communication*

---

[213] WSJ Moneybeat - Buffett Reminds His Top Managers: Reputation Is Everything (Dec 2014)

*or commerce and would be increasingly abandoned by consumers and
enterprises. Cyberspace would no longer be divided between attack-
ers and defenders but between predators and prey."* **World Economic
Forum** [214]

In this world, health data is highly prized and targeted for both its depth
and duration—which is literally lifelong.

The Internet I discovered haphazardly through a friend in 1996 is long gone,
and the risks associated with its use for research, shopping, entertainment,
and communication has grown exponentially. To date, most of that risk has
either been financial (think credit cards and Target) or embarrassing (think
Ashley Madison for adult affairs), but the amount of health data that's been
stolen over the last two years is staggering in comparison. We have yet to
see any real consequence to the sheer volume of health data that's been
stolen, but the clock has just started on its expiration date, which is a long
way out into the future for most. Not as much for us as adults, but certainly
for all the kids today.

As Malcolm Gladwell suggested at the Munk Debates, we've reconfigured
our risk in new ways that make it potentially more cataclysmic and no
industry or company is immune.

> *"We believe that data is the phenomenon of our time. It is the world's
> new natural resource. It is the new basis of competitive advantage, and
> it is transforming every profession and industry. If all of this is true –
> even inevitable – then cyber crime, by definition, is the greatest threat
> to every profession, every industry, every company in the world."* **Ginni
> Rometty** – Chairman, President and CEO of IBM [215]

We haven't seen it yet, but there's a "digital 911" on the path ahead. We can
only wonder what the scale and scope of it will be.

---

[214] World Economic Forum - Global Risks 2014 Report

[215] Forbes - IBM's CEO On Hackers: 'Cyber Crime Is The Greatest Threat To Every
Company In The World' (Nov 2015)

"You're seeing the early warning signs of something larger to come that's going to be disastrous and change how we live day-to-day. It's only a matter of time until we see a cataclysmic cyber attack. It'll be widespread and cause fear, panic and a sense of hopelessness." **David Kennedy** – Cybersecurity Consultant and former military hacker – U.S. Marines [216]

The Anthem breach of about 80 million records remains the largest data theft ever and left a lot of questions in its wake. Surprisingly—or perhaps not—the first answer delivered to investors and shareholders.

"Chris Rigg, an analyst with Susquehanna Financial Group, called Anthem's incident "unfortunate but manageable." J.P. Morgan Securities Analyst Justin Lake said in a note to investors that the data breach is not expected to hurt the company's lofty profit projections for 2015."[217]

The obvious lack of concern for our health data is a serious and troubling aspect of Casino Healthcare, but it is also reflective of the industry mindset. As long as the doors are open and the power on, there's really no financial risk to even the largest healthcare companies who continue to trivialize cyber security.

---

[216] CNN Money - Your worst hacking nightmares - and likely more to come (May 2015)

[217] Modern Healthcare: Huge data hack not expected to hurt Anthem's bottom line (02/2015)

"The enemy is fear. We think it is hate, but it is fear." **Ghandi**

XVI.

THE FOUR FEARS

So why are Americans so deathly afraid of a healthcare system like those in Canada, Germany, Japan, Germany—or really every other industrialized country? In some cases, it's because they don't know that over age 65, as a Medicare enrollee, they actually have a version that's similar to many of those countries. This story was recounted to noted economist Paul Krugman at The New York Times.[218]

> *"At a recent town-hall meeting in suburban Simpsonville, a man stood up and told Rep. Robert Inglis (R-S.C.) to 'keep your government hands off my Medicare.'"*
>
> *"I had to politely explain that, 'Actually, sir, your health care is being provided by the government',"* Inglis recalled. *"But he wasn't having any of it."*

Public sentiment often appears as hate and it's often fueled by cloudy and murky economic arguments against universal health coverage. Not surprisingly, those fanning the economic flames the loudest tend to have roots that can be traced back to consulting firms, payers, providers, lobbyists or drug and device manufacturers.

There are four fears that tend to dominate the debate toward a more global transformation like universal health coverage. Some of these fears can be traced back to the gaming and casino culture identified in the introduction of this book.

---

[218] New York Times: Why Americans hate single-payer insurance (07/2009)

The first fear is a false assumption (with big political support) that a system based on universal coverage is the same thing as a single payer system. It isn't. Germany, Switzerland, and The Netherlands are all great examples of universal coverage and multi-payer healthcare systems (many of which are heavily regulated, but private, insurance companies). Americans are quick to lump single-payer and universal health coverage together because it's convenient and much easier to argue a simple, binary comparison than a more complex, nuanced one.

The second fear is one of "rationing." This argument was originally ignited and set ablaze by Sarah Palin and her cavalier remarks about "death panels." The reality is that all healthcare (globally) is rationed, of course, but every other industrialized country starts with "universal coverage." America stands alone as the one industrialized country to base their healthcare system on "selective" health coverage.

The third fear is one of identity and is often referred to as "American exceptionalism." Here, the belief is that there is simply no other country on planet earth that can teach us anything. Those who identify with this thinking believe that our entire raison d'être is to be the world's beacon of shining success—in freedom, liberty, democracy and really everything—including a truly fictional belief that our healthcare system is the best in the world.

The fourth fear is more visceral and personal. It's the fear that paying for someone else's healthcare is a direct affront to one of our Founding Father documents—The Declaration of Independence.

> *"We hold these truths to be self-evident, **that all men are created equal**, that they are endowed by their Creator with certain unalienable Rights, that among these are Life, Liberty and the pursuit of Happiness."*

It's the great American myth—that all men are created equal because it says so in this founding document. We can (and should) strive for true equality in all forms of society, of course, but when it comes to healthcare—there are medical boundaries that often result in enormous challenges to the health cards we're dealt.

"The fundamental mythos of American culture, is that no matter how poor or humble your birth, you can through grit, spunk and hard work become wealthy and prosperous."

"On the face of it, and from the perspective of a class divided Europe, that seems incredibly noble and empowering. The idea that there is that much social mobility, that anyone can forge their own destiny is a powerful part of the American psyche. When it happens, it is an incredible thing. Something Americans can feel proud of."

"However, there is a dark side to this mythos. Which is this ... if anyone can win through hard work and effort, anyone who doesn't win, therefore deserves to be poor."

"At the core of all the anti-health care reforms is the single concept "why should I pay for the healthcare of those losers?"[219]

Collectively, these 4 fears are a significant impediment to the changes necessary to making our system safer, more affordable and more accessible.

Studies have tried to capture all the determinants of health—but they are weak attempts at mitigating the effect of the biggest single component of our health—the original lottery of life itself. One of the more detailed analyses was published in HealthAffairs in 2002 and led to this chart.[220]

[219] Quora Answer: Why do many Americans think that healthcare is not a right? (01/2011)

[220] HealthAffairs: The Case for More Active Policy Attention to Health Promotion (03/2002)

Determinants of Health

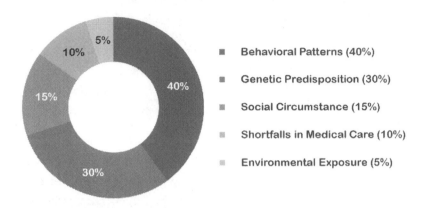

According to this chart—which is the result of a fairly rigorous scientific exercise—our genetic predisposition to premature death is approximately 30%, but even that figure is hard to support.

According to the CDC, the top ten clinical causes of death each year are:[221]

1. Heart disease: 611,105

2. Cancer: 584,881

3. Chronic lower respiratory diseases: 149,205

4. Accidents (unintentional injuries): 130,557

5. Stroke (cerebrovascular diseases): 128,978

6. Alzheimer's disease: 84,767

7. Diabetes: 75,578

8. Influenza and Pneumonia: 56,979

9. Nephritis, nephrotic syndrome, and nephrosis: 47,112

10. Intentional self-harm (suicide): 41,149

These ten clinical causes accounted for 1,910, 311 deaths in 2013.

---

[221] CDC: Leading Causes of Death (final data for 2013)

While cancer is the second most deadly disease, a recent study arrived at this startling conclusion relative to our individual ability to influence the occurrence of cancer with our own lifestyle choices.[222]

> *"These results suggest that only a third of the variation in cancer risk among tissues is attributable to environmental factors or inherited predispositions. The majority is due to "bad luck," that is, random mutations arising during DNA replication in normal, noncancerous stem cells."*

A more recent study suggests that this "bad luck" hypothesis is probably closer to 10-30%, but that's still a large percentage—especially in the realm of new and conflicting scientific evidence.[223] We may never know with great precision, but we do know it's a sizable percentage for each and every one of us.

Either way, the lottery of life can be tied directly to a significant rate of cancer which is the second leading cause of death.

Further, as a group, accidents, stroke and Alzheimer's account for about 18% of all deaths—and yet these too are health conditions for which we have limited capacity to influence directly.

Adding these random categories together, we arrive at 519,766 (or 27%) of the 1,910,311 deaths. Heart disease is much harder to pin down because there's simply a finite number of beats to each one.

Think that obesity is all diet, food and exercise? What if we have the science reversed and we're fighting the wrong battle in our war on obesity? What if obesity has nothing to do with eating too much? Those are the provocative

---

[222] Science: Variation in cancer risk among tissues can be explained by the number of stem cell divisions (01/2015)

[223] Nature: Substantial contribution of extrinsic risk factors to cancer development (01/2016)

questions that Dr. Peter Attia asked for his TEDMED 2013 talk.[224] As a clinician—he experienced this dilemma first hand.

> *"Despite exercising 3 or 4 hours every single day and following the food pyramid to the letter I gained a lot of weight and developed something called metabolic syndrome. I had become insulin resistant."*

What he didn't realize until later was that he was far from alone.

> *"About 30 million obese people don't have insulin resistance and about 6 million lean people are insulin resistant."*

From those statistics, it's clear that the science is far from resolved on this critically important—and global topic. The reality is that we continue to make assumptions about obesity for which the data either doesn't exist or is very limited. Since obesity is often the on-ramp to cancer, heart disease and even Alzheimer's, and given the lack of scientific data, the questions Dr. Attia asked during his talk demand scientific answers.

> *"What if obesity is the lesser of two metabolic evils? What if we have the cause and effect backward? What if insulin resistance is the cause of obesity? If obesity is nothing more than a proxy for metabolic illness — what good does it do us to punish those with the proxy?"*

Whatever our fears for dramatic change to the healthcare system, they are largely irrational and misplaced. We're afraid of making immediate changes to a system that, in fact, is a leading cause of death—preventable medical errors—and we're reluctant to provide health coverage to every American, even though our individual risk of contracting life-threatening diseases is attributable to either random cell mutations or the lottery of life. To reference the signature phrase of comedian Lewis Black, *"how dumb is that?"*

---

[224] TEDMED: Peter Attia (2013)

"Americans can always be counted on to do the right thing – after they've tried everything else."[225]

XVII.

THE FIRST STEP

The quote is often attributed to Winston Churchill, but unfortunately, there's no evidence that he ever said it. For that reason, it falls squarely under the rubric of Churchillian Drift, whereby a great quote by someone unknown is re-assigned to someone—like Churchill—who has more gravitas.

Whoever the author was, the quote remains popular in American politics and it's especially applicable to this chapter on our first step out of Casino Healthcare.

The Affordable Care Act—or simply Obamacare—began as a really big swing at healthcare reform. It was signed into law in 2010, and while it remains the law of the land, it's been challenged numerous times, in numerous ways. In January of this year, the House voted for the 62nd time to repeal Obamacare and this time the measure passed with a vote of 240 to 181.

This latest skirmish is as close to the repeal of Obamacare that the GOP will likely ever get and the true and only intent of the bill was purely symbolic. In the end, the GOP has a lot more to do than just oppose legislation; they have to propose legislation.

The bill (H.R. 132) to repeal Obamacare was submitted on January 6th, vetoed by the President on January 8th, and on January 10th, House Speaker Paul Ryan was questioned by Face The Nation host John Dickerson.[226]

---

[225] NPR: A Churchill 'Quote' That U.S. Politicians Will Never Surrender (10/2013)

[226] CBS News - Face the Nation: Interview with Speaker Ryan (01/2016)

John Dickerson: *You said you wanted the Republicans to offer an alternative to the President - one of the first things you did this year though was offer that repeal - how is that an alternative?*

House Speaker Paul Ryan: *It's not - that's why we have to come up with an alternative - so you're right about that.*

Almost six years after Obamacare, the GOP has no alternative plan. They simply don't have one that can be assessed, discussed and debated. Their steadfast objective so far has been to repeal Obamacare as if it were as binary as Prohibition. One day it was illegal to drink—the next it wasn't. That's pretty easy for everyone to understand, but while trivializing healthcare to that level may well score some political points, it won't succeed with any legislative objective—especially when the legislative impact is as personal and financial as healthcare.

The challenge to proposing an alternative is enormous because there are no alternatives to the actuarial science of health insurance. The game of fabricating products with no coverage or denying coverage to those who were sick as a way to 'rig' the game officially ended—and that's a good thing because it brings us at least one step closer to reality. Like shooting fish in a barrel, it's easy to profit by attracting healthy people and eliminating sick ones, but it shouldn't be legal.

> *"By offering products with low price and minimal coverage, they could attract the healthy, and by rejecting applicants with pre-existing diseases, they could eliminate the sick. The ACA made both of these practices illegal."*[227]

If Obamacare did nothing else, that alone is a significant accomplishment that deserves to stand. It's a very real acknowledgement that actuarial science exists and that we have a moral obligation to use it.

---

[227] KevinMD.com: These are the reasons why health insurers have to change (01/2016)

In the end, Obamacare didn't solve all of our healthcare woes, but it did have 6 major accomplishments and many ancillary ones—mostly around extending health insurance coverage to the almost 60 million who were uninsured when Barack Obama took office in January of 2009. The major accomplishments were:

Federal mandate requiring individuals to buy insurance coverage—with escalating fines for those who wouldn't buy health insurance if they didn't have access to coverage through their employer.

1. Federal subsidies (based on self-reported income) for the purchase of health insurance.

2. A cap on insurance profits with a federal mandate that 80-85% of every premium dollar collected by insurance companies would be spent on actual healthcare delivery. Sales, marketing, profits and the administration of premiums and claims were tied to that remaining 15-20% maximum.

3. A federal mandate that every health insurance policy have 10 "essential benefits."

4. Made it illegal to deny health insurance coverage based on any "pre-existing" health condition.

5. Funded several experiments around new payment models designed to wean the system off of a billing mechanism known as "fee-for-service." The goal here is to shift the whole system from one of billable volume to one based on outcomes and value.

The business of selling health insurance was dramatically changed—overnight. An entire market of people without access to health insurance through an employer had an affordable alternative and they bought in.

The original legislation also included a sweeping expansion of Medicaid in all 50 states, but that was legally challenged and found to be unconstitutional by the Supreme Court. While many states elected to expand Medicaid coverage under generous federal subsidies anyway, many others didn't. As of

January, 2016, 32 states (including DC) elected to expand Medicaid, 3 states remain "under discussion," and 16 states have said 'no' to the expansion.

Peter Orszag—one of the original architects of Obamacare—described the three fundamental pillars of Obamacare this way:

> *"It was to expand insurance coverage to more Americans, have at least a neutral effect on the U.S. deficit, and contain health-care costs."*[228]

As it nears its 6th anniversary, and evidenced by polling data from Gallup, the effect of Obamacare on expanding insurance coverage—the first pillar—has been nothing short of spectacular.[229]

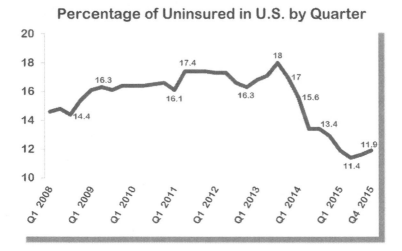

Percentage of Uninsured in U.S. by Quarter

A key weakness, however, has been and remains the third pillar—the actual cost of healthcare. Some are satisfied with controlling the growth of healthcare cost growth as seen in this chart.[230]

---

[228] BloombergView: Democrats Attack a Pillar of Obamcare (12/2015)

[229] Gallup: U.S. Uninsured Rate 11.9% in Fourth Quarter of 2015 (01/2016)

[230] Peterson-Kaiser: Health System Tracker (12/2015)

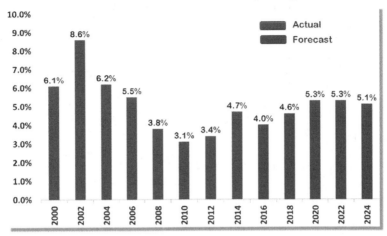

More important to average Americans, however, isn't the growth of health-care costs as much as it is the cost of actual healthcare as an increasing part of their budget. As evidenced in earlier chapters, the Milliman Medical Index suggests that we still have a long way to go in making both health coverage and healthcare actually affordable. That index suggests that healthcare represents a $900 line-item on the monthly budget of the average American family of 4 with employer-sponsored PPO coverage.

On the road ahead, many of the substantive effects of Obamacare are at risk of being degraded and the process of eroding core components continues unabated. As this writing, these same components designed to help cover the cost of implementing Obamacare will be delayed.

- The so-called 'Cadillac Tax'—designed to reign in extravagant employer sponsored health benefits.

- The medical device tax—designed to pay for elements of subsidizing health coverage.

- The health insurance tax—also designed to pay for elements of subsidizing coverage.

The short term effect isn't all that dramatic—maybe $40 billion over 2 years—but the prognosis for the taxes themselves and their contribution to the system overall isn't good.

> *"Peter Orszag, an economist who was Obama's first director of the Office of Management and Budget, said in an interview that "the big concern with delay is, it's not a delay, [but] it becomes a rolling permanent deferral." And that, he said, would undermine an essential "pillar" of the law: the goal of slowing the rise in health-care spending."*[231]

We've seen this exact movie before. In fact, the curtain finally came down on that production (known as the Sustainable Growth Rate – or SGR) just last year after a long and tedious 12-year congressional run. Passed in 1997, the intent of the SGR (as always) was to control the growth of costs paid to doctors through Medicare reimbursements. Initially, that cost growth was slow enough that the formula wasn't needed at all—until 2002. At that point, Congress did apply a 4.8% pay cut to physicians. From 2003 onward, however, legislation was passed each year to avoid similar pay cuts until finally, in 2015, legislation was passed that ended the SGR formula altogether. The risk of a sequel with taxes designed to support Obamacare is high.

States that refused to expand Medicaid—including states like Texas, Kansas and Missouri—appear to be dug in against expansion on strictly political, not economic reasons. Former Governor of Kansas, and now Secretary of Health and Human Services, Kathleen Sebelius leveled this harsh criticism at both Kansas and Missouri in a recent speech.

> *"Sebelius said Kansas and Missouri lawmakers' decisions not to expand Medicaid in their states hurt low-income women in particular. She said Kansas leaves more than $1 million on the table every day that Washington would otherwise spend to pay for Medicaid expansion. She said Missouri misses out on more than $5 million every day. 'It's*

---

[231] Washington Post: Congress to delay ACA's 'Cadillac' tax on pricey health plans until 2020 (12/2015)

*morally repugnant and economically stupid policy for both Kansas and
Missouri,' Sebelius said."[232]*

Other pieces of Obamacare highlight the enormous complexity of our fragmented healthcare system.

- So called "risk-corridors" as a federal subsidy to insurance companies for high risk populations in select parts of a city or state.

- Federally funded Consumer Operated and Oriented Plans (or
  Co-Op) that were an attempt to bring a nonprofit health insurance
  option to large cities—of which 12 (out of 23) have failed and
  defaulted on $1.2 billion in federal loans. Of the 11 remaining,
  only 2 have been able to break even.

- The question of whether or not plans sold on the Obamacare
  exchanges (either State run or through Healthcare.gov) are (or can
  be) profitable.

  *"The nation's largest health insurer warned Thursday that it may pull
  out of the Obamacare exchanges after 2016 – forcing more than a half
  million people to find other coverage – after low enrollment and high
  usage cost the company millions of dollars."[233]*

Most of the problems in healthcare stem from a lack of design for infrastructure that's at the very core of national health. Unlike other countries
that have standardized on universal health coverage, the U.S. has allowed
this critical infrastructure to simply evolve with piecemeal legislative
patches, some of which were accidental, through the decades. Legislation
like Medicare/Medicaid, COBRA, EMTALA, HIPAA, and PPACA were
all designed to patch glaring flaws with selective health coverage as they
appeared. None were designed to address healthcare as an entire system to
support an entire nation.

---

[232] KMBC.com: Sebelius blasts Kansas, MO. lawmakers on Medicaid funding, abor-
tion (12/2015)

[233] USA Today: UnitedHealth warns it may exit Obamacare plans (11/2015)

After years of contentious political wrangling, Medicare and Medicaid were finally added as amendments to the Social Security Act in 1965. Those were major milestones for granting healthcare to the poor and those over the age of 65, but it left employer sponsored insurance completely untouched. To this day we sort coverage by age (twice), employment, income, military service and exclude about 30 million Americans from coverage altogether (of which about 5 million are kids under the age of 18). As if that isn't complex enough—we add an annual enrollment process that churns both patients and networks of providers.

It was another 20 years before Ronald Reagan was able to sign the Consolidated Omnibus Budget Reconciliation Act of 1985—or COBRA. The primary goal with this was to provide optional health insurance coverage for workers who were between employers. It too left employer sponsored insurance (ESI) completely intact.

As a part of COBRA, congress also passed the Emergency Medical Treatment and Active Labor Act—or EMTALA. This was to ensure that emergency medical treatment would be provided "without regard to ability to pay." There was, of course, no federal or state funding for this, so hospitals that treat patients under EMTALA simply move the expenses into a bookkeeping category known as "uncompensated care." From here, the uncompensated care is shifted to all of us in the form of higher hospital charges—and premiums.

It would take another 25 years until President Obama would sign the Patient Protection and Affordable Care Act (PPACA) in 2010 as a way to address the large (and growing) number of people (almost 60 million) who were uninsured. A key element of Obamacare—mandating Medicaid expansion across all 50 states—was later invalidated by the Supreme Court. Once again, employer sponsored insurance was untouched.

Unlike other government functions, the importance of healthcare is emphasized in this quote by Senator Hubert Humphrey. The quote is actually inscribed on the wall at the entrance to the building that houses the

Department of Health and Human Services in Washington, D.C. That building also bears his name.

> *"The moral test of government is how it treats those who are in the dawn of life, the children; those who are in the twilight of life, the aged; and those in the shadows of life, the sick, the needy and the handicapped."*[234]

In almost every way, education and healthcare are the logical bookends of a society. It's the moral role of a democratically elected Government to field these infrastructure challenges directly—because of their sheer cost, scale and benefit to society. For all its bravado and bluster around "disruption," Silicon Valley isn't remotely capable of making systemic changes to infrastructure like education or healthcare on a national scale.

> *"I'm sure nobody wants to hear this and I'll be viciously attacked for suggesting it, but despite the constant refrain from entrepreneurs that they're trying to change the world, startups rarely do anything significantly world-changing. Really big paradigm shifting developments are so costly and require such a long term outlook that they essentially have to be disconnected from the profit requirement."*[235]

Francisco Dao is right—and we know it. Drug discovery may well be the lone exception for healthcare, but it too must be regulated for safety and (at some point) pricing value. It too must be held accountable for the record profits it logically deserves for finding cures.

Similar to prior legislation, however, patches like Obamacare can only go so far. We can only gamify actuarial math for so long. Healthcare reform needs to go beyond simply accurate financial math and into transparent cost accounting. Making money in healthcare is rarely a big challenge or risk, but how those efforts translate into savings that benefit all of us is always a big question.

---

[234] The Hubert H. Humphrey Building (HHS Headquarters), Washingtong, D.C.
[235] Pando: Why startups rarely change the world - Francisco Dao (08/2013)

It's conceivable that our dysfunctional system could withstand one of the many sizable flaws described in previous chapters, but the cumulative effect is so corrosive—it can only be categorized as legalized extortion. That may be perfectly acceptable for weekend gamblers visiting Caesars in Las Vegas because there are occasional winners, but the gamification of healthcare should be considered a criminal activity when it's applied to the health of a nation.

Certainly Obamacare changed the rules of coverage, subsidized millions to get coverage, and bought time, but it did nothing to solve for the 800-pound elephant in the room—cost.

By any measure, Obamacare has been successful. It has and will continue to save lives by correcting some of the glaring and egregious sins of the past, but it won't be enough. Health coverage is a big step out of Casino Healthcare, but it's only one step. More steps will be needed and should be expected. We're not remotely done with healthcare reform. In every technical and legal way possible, we've just begun. Politicians and political parties have to propose legislation—not simply oppose it.

Will Obamacare be repealed? It's a popular political argument for some—and a prayer for others—but the reality of its success makes repeal unlikely. It's legally possible, of course, but not likely.

> *"I think it cannot be repealed for a whole variety of reasons. First, almost every part of the healthcare sector – including hospitals and pharmaceutical companies – has built its entire strategy around the direction that ACA is taking the country. So I think that repeal would face resistance from almost every player in the marketplace. Second, and I think this is less understood from people not in government, is that you'd have a huge budget problem. This was true after ACA was first passed, and is even more true now. ACA creates budget surpluses and you cannot fill that big hole easily without raising taxes or doing other things you're opposed to. Third, you'd have to kick 15 million or so people off their healthcare insurance. Remember when the GOP was so upset that people had to change plans because theirs was canceled? Well, that was*

around 500,000 people. This would be 15 million. I don't think that's viable. **Zeke Emanuel** – *Obamacare Architect"*[236]

There will absolutely be additional healthcare legislation on the road ahead, but Obamacare isn't remotely like Prohibition. I believe it's here to stay as the first big step out of Casino Healthcare.

---

[236] Fortune: Obamacare Architect Zeke Emanuel Has A New Job (01/2016)

"Of all the forms of inequality, injustice in healthcare is the most shocking and inhuman." **Martin Luther King, Jr.**[237]

XVIII.

THE ROAD AHEAD

Martin Luther King, Jr. was right with this proclamation when he made it fifty years ago at the Medical Committee for Human Rights meeting on March 25, 1966. We can—and logically should—debate monetary inequality, but healthcare inequality truly is the most shocking and inhuman. It not only foundational to life, liberty, and the realistic pursuit of happiness, but it's also the backbone of a thriving society and economy.

Many major industrialists—from Henry Ford to Mark Zuckerberg—recognize the importance of a healthy workforce with direct benefits to their bottom line. One of the top ranked companies to work for has consistently been SAS, which was founded by James Goodnight in 1976. One of the hallmarks of his personal success as a tech titan and a founding principle of the company was the creation and integration of a healthcare facility directly into the sprawling campus headquarters in Cary, North Carolina.

> *"95% of my assets drive out the gate every evening. It's my job to maintain a work environment that keeps those people coming back every morning."* **James Goodnight** – *Founder SAS*

What should we expect for the road ahead now that Obamacare has taken a first and bold step toward healthcare reform? While we now know that Obamacare is a first step, what are some of the others that we should anticipate? One of the largest, by far, that is a direct threat to the unraveling of

---

[237] Huffington Post: Tracking Down Martin Luther King, Jr's Words on Health Care (01/2013)

Obamacare is cost. As the Milliman Medical Index highlights, we have not solved this and it is truly unsustainable.

One of the better summaries for the cost trajectory was suggested by long-time healthcare consultant and writer Paul Keckley in one of his weekly newsletters (bold emphasis mine).

> *"The CMS Office of the Actuary forecast is for health costs to increase at least 5.6% annually for the next decade due to increased utilization by those newly insured and expansion of Medicare enrollment, and the soaring costs of drugs. At the same time, the economy will likely grow at 3-3.5%, and inflation will average a 2-2.5% annual jump given the posture of the Federal Reserve toward our long term fiscal policy.* **So healthcare will consume more of the economy: that means higher insurance premiums for companies that offer coverage, less discretionary spending for their employees who see higher co-pays and deductibles, increased numbers of uninsured who can't afford coverage and a vigorous public debate about the next chapter in health reform."**[238]

Along with Paul's assessment at the end of 2015 was a poll of 1,004 Americans by Princeton Survey Research Associates International.[239] The poll was conducted in September of 2015 – and shows clearly just how divided we are across three critical questions.

1. How do you feel about your health insurance situation compared to 12 months ago?

    o   66% - about the same

    o   19% - worse

    o   14% - better

2. Would you keep or repeal Obamacare?

---

[238] Paul Keckley: Special Edition - In Health Reform 2.0 (12/2015)

[239] Slideshare: A Princeton Survey - America's Attitudes & Beliefs About Obamacare (10/2015)

- o   45% - keep in place
- o   44% - repeal it
- o   8% - don't know

3. How important will a candidate's views on Obamacare be to your vote in the 2016 Presidential election?

     - o   41% - very important
     - o   33% - somewhat important
     - o   11% - not too important
     - o   10% - not at all important
     - o   2% - don't know
     - o   1% - don't plan on voting

Given the presidential election cycle ahead, this last one is particularly insightful. A whopping 74% of Americans believe that a candidate's view of Obamacare will be an important consideration for the presidential election in November.

Another poll, also in the fall of 2015, by Kaiser Family Foundation spoke to the growing national anxiety around skyrocketing drug costs.[240]

The Public's Top Three Health Care Priorities

#1 – Making sure that high-cost drugs for chronic conditions are affordable to those who need them – 77%

#2 – Government action needed to lower prescription drug prices 63%

#3 – Making sure health plans have sufficient provider networks – 58%

In an earlier chapter I recounted the very real healthcare stories of four unique and courageous patients. I'll close this chapter—and the book—with one more: the story of Edna Rigss.

---

[240] Kaiser Health Tracking Poll: October 2015

Edna's story was recounted by Otis Brawley, the Chief Medical Officer of the American Cancer Society, in his book, "How We Do Harm."[241] The opening chapter of his book is called simply, "Chief Complaint" and it chronicles the arrival of Edna, a trim, middle-aged black woman, to the emergency room of Grady Memorial, a "safety net" hospital in Atlanta, Georgia.

> *"She walks through the emergency room doors sometime in the early morning. In a plastic bag, she carries an object wrapped in a moist towel.*

> *"She is not bleeding. She is not in shock. Her vital signs are okay. There is no reason to think that she will collapse on the spot. Since she is not truly an emergency patient, she is triaged to the back of the line, and other folks, those in immediate distress, get in for treatment ahead of her. She waits on a gurney in a cavernous green hallway."*

> *"The 'chief complaint' on her chart at Grady Memorial Hospital, in downtown Atlanta, might have set off a wave of nausea at a hospital in a white suburb or almost any place in the civilized world. It reads, 'My breast has fallen off. Can you reattach it?' She waits for at least four hours – likely five or six. The triage nurse doesn't seek to determine the whereabouts of the breast. Obviously, the breast is in the bag."*

The medical term is automastectomy, which is when the breast falls off by itself. According to Dr. Brawley, this is seen a "couple of times a year" at places like Grady, "often enough to be taken in stride."

Edna actually had insurance through her employer—the phone company—but the cost kept escalating. At $3,000 a year, it became too expensive relative to her income to keep, so it lapsed. Edna Riggs didn't survive the cancer that caused her breast to fall off. She died about twenty months after walking into Grady Memorial. She was 55.

For reasons like Edna's story—and millions of others—our national debate for systemic healthcare reform continues. Obamacare is a new dividing line

---

[241] Amazon Books: How We Do Harm - A Doctor Breaks Ranks About Being Sick in America (10/2012)

between those who say reform has already gone too far, and those of us who say it's a single step out of Casino Healthcare.

The debate is often cloaked in one or more myths. Speaking at the 20th International Forum on Quality and Safety in Healthcare in London this last spring, Don Berwick summarized the eight myths that he argues we need to abandon.[242]

1. Incentives Will Save Us

2. "Skin in the game" Will Save Us

3. Measurement Will Save Us

4. Accountability Will Save Us

5. Standards Will Save Us

6. Markets Will Save Us

7. Technology Will Save Us

8. Health Care Will Save Us

Sadly, even with Obamacare, we haven't made much progress on the healthcare injustice that Martin Luther King, Jr. identified over 50 years ago. Today we have roughly 30-35 million Americans without healthcare insurance—and roughly another 30 million that are underinsured. That means that a major healthcare event would likely bankrupt them. As it is, the average American family budget is far more brittle than most realize.

> *"If someone encounters a significant, unexpected expense outside his or her budget, such as an emergency room visit or a car repair, only 38 percent of respondents said they could cover it with cash they have on hand in a savings account or checking account."*[243]

While it's tempting to think that insurance coverage alone is sufficient to make healthcare costs affordable, recent studies suggest otherwise. Many who managed to buy insurance are quick to find that all costs are not

---

[242] Twitter: Natalie Silvey tweet of Don Berwick slide (04/2015)

[243] Bankrate: Budgets can crumble in times of trouble (01/2015)

covered. High deductible health plans, co-pays and expensive prescription drugs continue to erode coverage and undermine incremental reform like Obamacare. Escalating costs continue to create an ever increasing group of uninsured and underinsured.

> *"Overall, about a quarter (26 percent) of U.S. adults ages 18-64 say they or someone in their household had problems paying or an inability to pay medical bills in the past 12 months. Though certain groups are more likely than others to report such problems, the survey finds that people from all walks of life can and do experience difficulty paying medical bills."*[244]

According to a study published in early 2014, 56 million Americans under the age of 65 "will have trouble paying medical bills," and are the leading cause of personal bankruptcy in the U.S. [245]

Healthcare inequality in America isn't just an injustice as Martin Luther King, Jr. suggests, it's an injustice at scale.

It's easy to see the lottery of life through all the stories in this—and dozens of other books. Edna, Anna, Hugo, Brooke, and Eric are a tiny sample to be sure, but through them it's easy to see just how a serious health condition—either lifelong or life–ending—can happen to any one of us. With the passage of age, the actuarial math almost guarantees it.

Ultimately, of course, death in inevitable, but access to basic, affordable health care shouldn't be comparable to playing roulette or some other casino game—and certainly not as the foundational infrastructure for the health of a nation. The national highway system, GPS technology, landing a man on the moon, and the very internet itself were all national infrastructure investments that continue to pay big dividends. Shouldn't healthcare be on the scale of one of those priorities?

---

[244] Kaiser Family Foundation: The Burden of Medical Debt (01/2016)

[245] NerdWallet: NerdWallet Health Finds Medical Bankruptcy Accounts for Majority of Personal Bankruptcies (03/2014)

The challenge on the road ahead is removing as much risk as we can from our lottery of life in ways that are both equitable and don't wind up bankrupting each of us financially. For a system that includes 320 million people, across 50 United States—that's a tall order—especially when we consider all of the odds stacked against us.

So what's the answer—what's the "road ahead?" There are really only 2 steps ahead and both are inevitable. We must accelerate their adoption.

1) End the "iron-triangle-of-healthcare" and convert the 4-party system of employer sponsored insurance to a 3-part one—patient, provider and payer.

2) End the other perversion that is unique to America—selective health coverage. It logically follows that with a single tier of universal coverage, tiered (and wildly variable) pricing on delivery is also eliminated.

The timeline is unknown and debatable, but the ultimate outcome is fairly predictable. We're on a trajectory to that destination now. Obamacare will continue to be tested and challenged, but it's another major milestone on the path to the second step—universal health coverage. That may not be single-payer, because as we've seen through other countries, multi-payer is a very viable alternative as well.

Testing and challenging Obamacare is healthy because we need new models of healthcare delivery. That debate should logically include broader coverage in every direction and new ways to pay for value over volume. Obamacare set a new and historic benchmark for the sheer number of Americans with healthcare insurance, and that needs to be applauded, but like all markets, those impressive numbers can just as easily be reversed. There is a very real risk of losing the hard-fought ground that Obamacare ushered in. The small, but perceptible, uptick of uninsured in the final quarter of 2015 is noteworthy as a way to highlight the economic fact that every trend is reversible.

As long as we perpetuate a casino mindset to the whole system, things like selective, tiered coverage with annual renewals and variable costs, the system will struggle under the weight of 320 million Americans aging at an accelerated rate for the next 15-20 years.

Beyond the obvious benefits of Obamacare, is a more nuanced prescription. Obamacare does represent an important milestone and lynchpin for many reasons—and at least two in particular:

1) Like Medicare in 1965—once a significant social benefit is delivered—it's difficult to take back.

2) The law effectively tilted us away from selective health coverage toward universal health coverage.

Tilting toward universal coverage is a great thing, but cost weighs heavily on the risk of reversal.

While there are many who vehemently oppose the idea, the logic for universal coverage is both financially and morally sound. It is also why literally every other industrialized country has standardized on this form of health coverage.

The time has long since passed to end the search for the winning lottery ticket that can magically contort actuarial math. That Powerball number simply doesn't exist and it's time for those hopes and prayers to end. Actuarial math always wins and that math for healthcare means that the largest possible pool of coverage—literally everyone—is also the most fiscally sound. It's a crude example, but the math around the polar extremes is easy to understand. Using $5,000 as the theoretical cost for a healthcare procedure —any procedure—here are the polar extremes.

$$N = 1 = \$5,000$$

$$N = 320 \text{ million} = \$0.000015625$$

Every other industrialized country has effectively chosen the latter and while America isn't the former, we continue to try to make the N=1 work. We're stuck somewhere in the middle. The gamification of health coverage—by employment, age, military service and then sorted through a byzantine process of annual enrollment—is costing a fortune.

For those who argue we can't afford universal health coverage, the rebuttal is simple. Our current trajectory is unsustainable. We can no longer afford selective health coverage. The only effective counterbalance to a resource that's limited in supply is pooling demand—not just selectively, but as large as possible.

We already have the prototype for universal health coverage and it's called Medicare because every citizen over the age of 65 is covered. Not surprisingly, proponents of universal health coverage here in the U.S. often refer to universal health coverage as Medicare-for-All, but we also need to remember that the importance of universal coverage trumps the payment mechanism. Single payer may be desirable, but there are multi-payer alternatives like Germany, The Netherlands and Switzerland that warrant consideration and debate. They may be more palatable for our culture and it accelerate the path to universal coverage.

There have been state-led attempts at forging a universal health coverage system in the past, and a universal-coverage, single-payer initiative in Colorado will be voted on by the people in that state in November of 2016.

Without going into a long history of the previous attempts, I doubt that this latest one in Colorado will succeed: As Florida Governor Rick Scott so eloquently suggested, the healthcare industry isn't remotely interested in reducing revenue and profits, and they're very well financed. That financing makes it relatively easy to block any legislative attempt to change.

This brings us to the very heart of our healthcare dilemma. Like a lot of problems in the country—including education, energy, and Wall Street reform—healthcare is a big intractable one. Individually and collectively, these are all big problems, but they aren't the first problem.

> *"Again and again, what America wants, Congress doesn't do – because the citizens who fund elections are represented and the rest of us are not. Every issue – from climate change to gun safety, from Wall Street [and healthcare] reform to defense spending – is blocked by this fundamental*

problem: Congress does not represent the people. The solution is to fix our democracy first." **Lawrence Lessig,** *Harvard Law Professor*[246]

Relative to the political influence of the few—and wealthy—here's a statistic that's truly hard to comprehend. A mere 132 Americans—representing 0.000042% of the entire population—contributed 60% of all SuperPAC money during the 2012 presidential election cycle.

As a problem, campaign financing isn't new. Its influence was evident in this quote from William M. (Boss) Tweed, a New York State Senator in the late 1800s:

"I don't care who does the electing so long as I get to do the nominating."

While the American public is content to focus on the hoopla of the general election in November 2016, it's the huge financial interests that align around the real power—not in the election, but in the nomination—and healthcare has had a disproportionate influence in that game.

The argument here isn't about the inequality of wealth; it's about the fundamental equality of citizenship. Over the course of seventeen years (1998 – 2015), of the fifteen industries that contributed over $1 billion to political lobbying efforts nationally, healthcare interests have represented almost $8 billion (or about 33% of the $24.5 billion total).[247]

---

[246] Lessig2016: Fix Democracy First Campaign (11/2015)

[247] OpenSecrets.org: Lobbying - Top Industries from 1998 - 2015

Political Lobbying – Top 15 Industries	
(1998 – 2015)	
Pharmaceutical/Health Products:	$3,201,510,687
Insurance:	$2,234,393,387
Electric Utilities:	$2,040,702,304
Electronic Mfg & Equipment:	$1,853,271,085
Business Associations:	$1,842,908,662
Oil & Gas:	$1,750,255,336
Misc Mfg & Distribution:	$1,442,304,755
Education:	$1,419,264,645
Hospitals / Nursing Homes:	$1,332,519,332
Telecom Services:	$1,291,783,209
Securities & Investment:	$1,287,877,075
Civil Servants / Public Officials:	$1,235,147,415
Real Estate:	$1,233,235,907
Health Professionals:	$1,221,036,450
Air Transportation:	$1,144,829,349
Total:	$24,531,039,598
Total Healthcare related (~33%):	$7,989,459,856

For those who may think this will somehow change for the upcoming 2016 election cycle, the evidence suggests otherwise. During 2015, healthcare interests increased their political lobbying dollars from 33% of the top fifteen industries to a more robust 36%.

Political Lobbying – Top 15 Industries	
(2015)	
Pharmaceutical/Health Products:	$235,107,261
Insurance:	$155,805,113
Oil & Gas:	$128,645,515
Business Associations:	$128,318,664
Electronic Mfg & Equipment:	$121,801,510
Electric Utilities:	$117,762,016
Misc Mfg & Distribution:	$103,780,058
Securities & Investments:	$96,195,738
Health Professionals:	$95,992,515
Hospitals / Nursing Homes:	$91,274,306
Telecom Services:	$88,771,758
Air Transportation:	$80,642,628
Real Estate:	$77,073,493
Education:	$76,012,058
Defense Aerospace:	$73,820,775
Total:	$1,671,003,408
Total Healthcare related (~35%):	$578,179,195

In fairness, the category of insurance (always #2) represents all types of insurance—not just healthcare—but the largest component of that is most certainly healthcare. Certainly life, auto, property and casualty have lobbying interests as well, but they pale in comparison to the trillions of dollars flowing through health insurance annually.

The only institution that has the capacity to reverse these heavily entrenched financial interests is the federal government, but regulatory capture presents a moral dilemma for government officials who enjoy the trappings of power and rely on the 1% for campaign funding. This is the real dilemma that we face as a country and the very health of our nation hangs in the balance. Former U.S. Senate Majority Leader Tom Daschle described the challenge he's seen firsthand.[248]

- Congressmen (and women) spend about 30 hours a week raising money.

- The airplane has changed the actual function of Government. Congressmen leave on Thursday afternoon and return on Tuesday—so we try to run the Government on one day—Wednesday.

It's not just the corruptible influence of money in politics; it's the effect of time on the very role itself.

Implementing universal coverage isn't really a matter of *if*, but *when*. How we pay for that is a debate we need to have, but the idea that universal coverage can only be delivered via a single-payer system is inaccurate. Those who claim single-payer and universal coverage to be one and the same are arguing a political agenda, not fact.

In the end, for a country of our size and wealth, it's not really an economic debate at all – it's a moral one. Our history is rich with big, expensive projects that benefitted not just the U.S. but all of mankind. After toiling away in a lab for 7 years, Jonas Salk discovered a vaccine for polio—and then gave it away. Government research invented the internet—and then gave the keys to commercial interests. The same is true for Global Positioning Satellite (GPS) and countless other scientific and technology innovations that have benefitted the whole world.

Relative to healthcare, there are viable alternatives outside of single-payer that are more logical for our cultural sensibilities. We all want choice. We can still have choice under a system of universal coverage, but we have to separate the political lie that universal coverage is single payer. It isn't.

---

[248] Harvard T.H. Chan: Voices in Leadership video - Tom Daschle (03/2016)

The decision is not whether we will ration care. The decision will be whether we ration care with our eyes open. **Don Berwick,** *MD*[249]

The road ahead is actually fairly certain. We will end the accident of history known as employer-sponsored insurance and we will implement a form of universal health coverage, and not because they are the morally-desirable options—which they are—but because they are in our long-term economic interest. The existing model in use today has become both unstable and unsustainable. We're just taking the long and scenic route to the only viable alternative to selective health coverage.

Churchill may not have said it, but we do gravitate to the right thing, but as the quote suggests, only after we've tried everything else. We're still trying to keep Casino Healthcare open, but the game is really up. We've optimized healthcare for revenue and profits. The time has come to optimize it for safety and quality. That will be neither easy nor quick, but the health of an entire nation now depends on it.

---

[249] BrainyQuote: Don Berwick